Dog

Tricks

Fun and games for your clever canine

Mary Ray • Justine Harding

hamlyn

First published in Great Britain in 2005 by
Hamlyn, a division of Octopus Publishing Group Ltd
2–4 Heron Quays, London E14 4JP

ISBN-13: 978 0 600 59460 4
ISBN-10: 0 600 59460 2

A CIP catalogue record for this book is available
from the British Library

Printed and bound in China

10 9 8 7 6 5 4 3 2 1

Contents

Why teach tricks?

Teaching your dog tricks is fun. It is rewarding, entertaining and gives you the chance to show others just how smart your dog is. Your dog will benefit physically and mentally, and the pair of you will get the chance to build a better relationship. You will find that your understanding of one another improves, along with the trust between you. In short, you and your dog will enjoy each other's company more.

Tricks are simply an extension of the training that responsible owners already do with their pets. It just takes your dog's skills to a higher level. If you watch dogs playing together, you will see them naturally performing many of the moves that are taught to be performed on cue in this book. When dogs are kept alone, these behaviours tend to be lost, but they can be triggered again with training.

Dogs are very intelligent and need to have their minds occupied, but unfortunately they are often not challenged enough and will find their own ways to stimulate their brains. This is when behavioural problems can arise due to boredom and frustration. By teaching tricks, you can give your dog plenty to think about and so help prevent these issues from developing – or even help solve those that are already there. As the saying goes, the dog is man's best friend, but if he is taught some basic skills and tricks, he will become an even better friend.

But, of course, you don't get all these benefits without a little investment. You need to spend a little time with your dog each day to get the best results. Just five minutes here and there, and longer sessions when you can fit them in, will be enough to see results. If you have any hiccups along the way, simply refer to the 'training checklist' on page 19 to help overcome any minor difficulties before they become bigger problems that will be harder to resolve.

Dog-owning is all about building a rewarding relationship for you both.

What's in it for your dog?
- Quality time with you
- A chance to really use his brain
- Improvement in physical fitness and suppleness
- Lots of fun and treats
- A happy owner

What's in it for you?
- Quality time with your dog
- The reward of seeing your dog's enjoyment at showing off his talents
- The surprise of learning just how smart your dog is
- Lots of fun
- A more responsive, obedient, happy dog

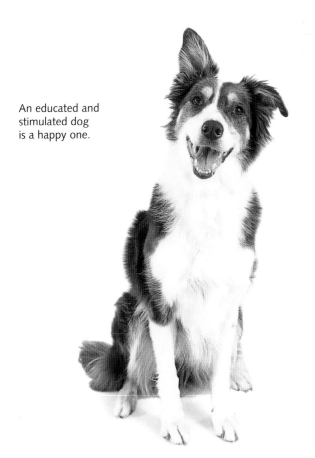

An educated and stimulated dog is a happy one.

Praise, not punishment

Years ago, tricks were seen as bad things to teach to animals – not because of the tricks themselves, but because of the way they were taught. Today, the modern training methods recommended in this book mean that no punishment is ever used, only rewards and praise. Plus, good trainers learn to make the most out of the behaviours that each individual dog naturally shows. It is not surprising then that, by using this approach, dogs thoroughly enjoy learning new tricks and are eager to show what they can do in the hope of getting another treat.

Teamwork gets the best results.

Assess for success

So you and your dog are keen to start learning some smart moves. You may even already have your eye on a few tricks that you feel are particularly impressive. That's great – with that enthusiasm you'll go far. However, your particular dog should also have an influence on the tricks you choose and how you teach them. Dogs come in all shapes, sizes, types, breeds, ages and abilities. While nearly all are capable of learning tricks, your training will be much more successful if you take these characteristics into account from the outset.

Age

Contrary to the adage that you can't teach an old dog new tricks, in fact, *no* dog is too old to learn new tricks. Consider what training he has done already, as well as his fitness and health. For example, a dog that is stiff in his hips and has had only limited training won't achieve reversing backwards (see page 86) as easily as giving a paw (see page 36). Equally, young dogs and puppies will not be physically or mentally mature enough for some moves, especially those involving jumping or being in an upright position. Instead, concentrate on other tricks for now and build up from there.

Type or breed

Your dog's type will also affect which tricks he excels at and which he finds harder. For example, small dogs usually find upright tricks like standing on their hindlegs very easy. But there are always exceptions to the rule. One particular 12-year-old Bulldog, for instance, easily does high fives (see page 44) and creeps backwards, despite his natural shape suggesting that he would find both of these actions hard to do.

Border Collies are often thought of as the crème de la crème of dogs for specialist training due to their intelligence and willingness to please. But although they are very clever, being an 'eye' breed, Collies like to be actually shown what is required. Other breeds or crossbreeds are often better at thinking for themselves. So whatever you dog's shape, breed or type, have a go – you'll probably be surprised at what you can both achieve with a bit of work.

Left- or right-pawed?

Just like humans, dogs tend to be right- or left-handed, so will find some tricks easier to do on one side than the other. Watch how your dog moves and see which side he naturally favours. By knowing if your dog is right- or left-handed, you can then help him to learn new things more easily by always starting on his 'easier' side. Also, by teaching him tricks on both sides, he will become more balanced and supple.

Early training will be through play and develops as your puppy matures.

Whatever size or shape your dog is, there will be tricks to suit him.

Keep playtime and lessons separate initially, to save frustration for you both.

Where to train your dog

You can easily teach your dog tricks at home and in your garden, and as you and he get more confident, practise out on walks. At home your dog should be relaxed and confident and so ready to learn. Always choose a room with a non-slip, soft floor, such as carpet, so that your dog feels that he has a good footing and is comfortable if you ask him to lie down. Make sure you have plenty of clear floor space so that your dog can move around confidently, without colliding with furniture, and can easily find treats thrown to him. Choose quiet, confined spaces to begin with to help your dog keep focused on you. As he improves, practise your tricks where there are distractions.

What you need

To do any job well, you need the right tools, and dog training is no exception. You are likely to have quite a few of the things you'll need already, while others you won't need until you start to do the more advanced tricks.

Collar and lead
You will require a lead only if your dog initially has to work on his basic training (see page 20). Most tricks are best taught off lead. Choose a full leather collar of a thickness to suit your dog's neck and adjust it so that you can just fit two fingers under it. The lead needs to sit in your hand comfortably, and be thick and long enough for the size of your dog, but not so long that you cannot easily take up the slack.

Dog toys
You probably already have a selection of dog toys and a good idea of what your dog likes. Tug toys are good for training, as long as your dog enjoys them, as you can play with him but still get the toy back readily. Keep a couple of favourite toys for training sessions only.

Treats
Choose a mix of high-value treats that your dog loves. Usually cooked meat, cheese or frankfurters are the most prized. Find out more about choosing and using treats on page 12.

Treat bag or pot
A bag that fits round your waist is ideal. You can get treats for your dog easily, wherever you are, while keeping your hands free. Alternatively, have a full treat pot nearby.

Clicker
This is a small, hand-held device that has a metal tongue that emits a 'click-click' sound when pressed. It is used to tell your dog when he has done the right thing (see page 16). A box clicker has the tongue set within it and is operated with your thumb, while the button clicker has a push button, so can be operated under your foot.

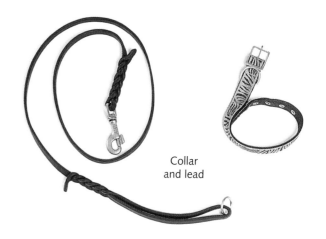

Collar and lead

Treats

Dog toys

Target stick

Clickers

Basket

Ball

Poles and cones

Puppy pen

Puppy pen

This is a multi-panelled, hinged wire fence that can be arranged in a number of different shapes. Although designed for keeping puppies out of mischief, it is ideal for teaching certain more advanced tricks, too. However, you can also improvise with what you may have available.

Target markers and sticks

Some tricks can be taught more effectively using a 'target', which gives the dog a clear point to touch or follow. A target marker is a small mat, plastic lid or flat piece of wood usually used to position a dog (see pages 101 and 103). A target stick, like the one pictured (see left), is an extendable wand. With the aid of different 'attachments' on the end, such as a small ball or a flat, rectangular piece of plastic or wood (see pages 101 and 102), you can teach your dog to move in new ways.

Poles and jumps

If you want to teach weaving, pole-related tricks or jumping, you'll need these. You can buy specially designed poles and cone bases from suppliers of equipment for agility, which have a dual-purpose – the poles can stand upright in a cone base for weaving or be laid horizontally across two cones to form jumps. You can make your own poles for weaving from a lightweight broom handle set into a heavy block, so that it cannot easily be knocked over. In contrast, when making your own jumps, you need to use something that can easily be knocked down without causing any discomfort to your dog, such as a bamboo cane.

Props

In the book, a hoop, cane, basket, skateboard, blanket, ball and wastebasket are used, but you can adapt the tricks to suit what you have to hand. Let your imagination run wild!

Teaching tricks using food

Most dogs love food and will do almost anything to get it! Even dogs who aren't bothered about treats will become much keener once 'high-value' foods are used and given in proportion to what they are being asked to do. Just like us, dogs will only work if their 'pay' is worth it.

For training, 'real' food is the best, as it is very desirable to your dog. Always select food that doesn't crumble and is visible if thrown to the floor, and cut it into thumbnail-sized cubes. Give any food the three-second test: can your dog – and does he want to – chew and swallow it in under three seconds? If not, it will have no value in training.

To maximize the effectiveness of your treats, make sure your dog hasn't just eaten before training and cut down his meals to allow for the food he will receive as rewards.

Using food to train

Food is used in two ways to teach your dog tricks. Firstly, it is a reward for doing the right thing. Give the treat straight after your dog does as you have asked, either directly from your hand or by throwing it to him. By throwing treats, you can reward your dog more quickly when he is at a distance to you and prevent him anticipating food always coming from your hand.

Most dogs are real 'foodies' and will happily work for treats as long as you pay well!

Top four training treats
1 Sausages
2 Frankfurters
3 Mild hard cheese
4 Lamb's liver

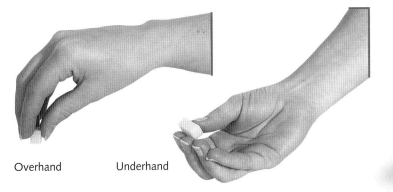

Overhand   Underhand

Secondly, food can be used to show your dog what you want – this is called luring. By holding a tasty treat in the tips of your fingers close to his nose, you can encourage him to follow your hand into the position or through the move you are teaching. Experiment with how your hand position affects your dog's movement. The position of his nose will determine the direction of the rest of his body. For example, if you encourage him to lift his nose high, his tail is likely to go down, so this will help you to ask him to sit. To help lure your dog successfully, practise both the overhand position (above left) and the underhand position (above right).

While luring can be used as a training method in itself, it is much more effective when used alongside clicker training (see page 16).

With food held in your fingertips, you can 'lure' your dog in any direction.

The right rewards

Many owners find that their dog works for them only if they have food. This is commonly due to dogs being expected to work for very little reward or having the reward cut out too quickly after they have learned something new. They will quickly work out whether you 'pay' well! Be generous with your treats, especially early on in training, so that your dog knows his effort is worthwhile. Then gradually, when he understands the trick and enjoys doing it, reduce the rewards, offer them more randomly or ask for more work in return. Keep him guessing what he is going to get.

🐾 Key points

● Luring requires your dog to watch the food, rather than to grab at it. Teach your dog not to snatch by holding the treat firmly between the tips of your fingers, so that he can smell it but not actually get it. Keep your hand still and wait until he stops biting at the treat. As soon as he pulls back slightly, give it to him. By repeating this, you will soon teach your dog that he gets the food more easily by being patient.

● Take care not to drop crumbs on the floor, as your dog will soon learn to look for 'freebies' rather than at you.

● Make sure you are always the best source of food around, then your dog will have no need to look anywhere else for treats.

Canine communication

Dogs are masters of body language, but sadly we humans are not. Owners are often convinced that they are telling their dog to do one thing, usually with their voice, but, in fact, their body position is saying the complete opposite.

To train your dog successfully, you need to tell him clearly and consistently what you want – the better at this you are, the quicker and easier he will learn. As well as using your voice and body language, communicate with him using facial expressions, touch, hand signals and, as you'll see throughout this book, the clicker (see page 16).

Body language

Dogs tune into your silhouette, so think about keeping your body shape clear. As you work your dog, always use the hand on the side closest to your dog to lure or signal, rather than crossing your arms over your body. Frequently, your dog won't actually be reading the signal you think you are giving him, but will take his cue from something much more subtle. Be aware, too, how your movement can affect your dog's – stepping into him will make him hesitant to come close to you again. Leaning over your dog

What barking means

Barking is frequently the response of a confused or frustrated dog. This is your dog asking for more clues as to what you want. Don't keep trying the same thing, but go back to the last step he understood. Then give him some further pointers to what you want now, checking that your signals are clear.

Always use the hand closest to your dog to lure or signal, to avoid confusion.

When training a small or young dog, get down to their level.

Key points

● A dog can perform a trick from a voice, hand or body signal.

● The movement you use initially to lure your dog will form the first visual cue.

● When the dog can do the trick following just your hand movement, add the verbal command you wish to use.

● Use verbal and visual cues together, so that your dog connects both to the trick.

● With practice, you will be able to get your dog to perform from just a voice command or just a visual signal. For very slick tricks, the visual cues may then be refined to tiny, almost invisible movements by gradually reducing the signal you give.

can make him feel threatened, especially with puppies or small dogs, so try kneeling down. Make sure you always allow your dog enough room to complete the move you are asking for.

Hand signals

When teaching a trick, use large movements to begin with and gradually reduce them. This will make the signals clear and easier for your dog to follow. If you want to use hand signals to cue your dog for a trick, they need to be distinct.

Voice

Think carefully about the verbal commands you use in order to avoid confusing your dog. Words can often sound similar, such as 'bow' and 'down'. Also, vary the tone of your commands – upwards-type moves are usually better given in a higher-pitched voice, while downward or lower moves can be given in lower tones.

Use big signals when teaching a trick before refining them to near invisible cues.

Introducing the clicker

If you are familiar with the traditional methods of dog training, prepare yourself for a new astonishing, rewarding and fun experience: clicker training. And don't be tempted to disregard it as a gimmick – even some highly sceptical professionals have been won round to the clicker approach after seeing what it can achieve. The method was originally developed by dolphin trainer Karen Pryor and it has since taken dog training on in leaps and bounds. But why is it so good? The five main reasons are:

1 Your dog quickly learns that each time he hears a click he will always gets a reward.
2 You can mark the exact behaviour you want your dog to repeat with a click.
3 The click remains consistent, so it is easy for your dog to understand.
4 The clicker provides a bridge between your dog's behaviour and the reward, as you can tell him he has done well even if you cannot give him a treat instantly. A click promises a reward. This is invaluable especially when your dog is at a distance from you or in the middle of a move that you don't want to interrupt with a treat.
5 Your dog is encouraged to think and work out for himself what you want – rather than just being taught parrot-fashion – so he will actively participate in and enjoy his lessons.

The clicker

Box clickers are the most common (see page 10) and work simply by pressing down the metal tongue in the centre with your thumb and releasing, which produces a 'click-click'. Always aim to hold the clicker in the hand away from your dog, with food treats in the hand closest to him. Avoid clicking close to your dog's ear.

Clicker training is all about letting your dog use his own brain and be part of the training process – this is what makes it so enjoyable. There is no punishment, just the opportunity to try again, or praise for doing the right thing, which creates confidence. Even the quietest, most retiring dogs that are normally far too shy to do anything in front of other people can become confident, responsive trick artists with clicker training – and the Sheltie pictured below is one such example, being transformed from the most reluctant performer to a dog willing to take part in dog-training demonstrations at Crufts.

Clicker training can boost a dog's confidence as well as their repertoire of skills.

While food is best for training many dogs, others just love their toys.

Clicking for tricks

All the tricks in this book follow this same basic training sequence which, once you and your dog have tuned into it, will get progressively easier.

LURE your dog so that he performs the DESIRED BEHAVIOUR for a trick.

CLICK! TREAT

PRACTISE until your dog can do the moves following your signals but without a lure.

Once your dog understands the trick, give him a VERBAL COMMAND.

CLICK! TREAT

PRACTISE so that your dog no longer needs your hand signals but performs the trick on just the voice commands.

Add a refined visual signal if desired.

Selective clicking

Once your dog understands that 'click' always means reward, you have a vast array of possibilities at your fingertips. For example, the clicker can be used to 'capture' natural behaviours, such as a leg stretch or a head shake. Simply wait for the behaviour to occur, click and treat, and your dog will quickly try to re-create what resulted in the reward. However, be aware that any behaviour occurring as you click may be reproduced by your dog. So, if you click him for wagging his tail but he barks at the same time, you may inadvertently encourage him to bark. Unwanted behaviours can simply be taken back out of your dog's repertoire by never clicking them again.

Clicking for tricks

So now you know what a clicker is and what it can offer to you and your dog, and better still, your enthusiasm for it is likely to grow as you see the results for yourself. However, first of all you need to teach your dog that the clicker is significant for him, too.

At the moment, a clicking sound will mean nothing to your dog, although he may look up to see what is making the noise. You need to teach him that the click is positive, rewarding and well worth responding to. From this simple but crucial lesson, the rest of your dog's training will begin to fall into place.

1 Call your dog to you and give him a few treats so that he knows you have them.

2 Hold the clicker in one hand and a treat in the other. Simply click and immediately afterwards give your dog a treat. Keep repeating this, aiming to click when your dog is looking at you – it won't take long before you'll see your dog thinking 'yippee' each time he hears a click and start watching you for the next piece of food.

3 You can then try throwing a piece of food on the floor. Click just before your dog eats it and then repeat.

4 Now test that your dog understands that clicks equal rewards. Choose a simple command that he already knows, such as 'sit'. Command 'sit', making a click as he does this, and reward once he's sitting. Then move away a few steps – he is likely to follow you for more treats. Again tell him to 'sit', click as he reaches a sit and reward. Move away once more, but this time say nothing – he should come and sit beside you of his own accord. Just click and treat. Well done – you are on your way.

Training checklist

As you try the tricks in this book, there will be times when things don't go quite according to plan. If ever there's a hiccup, take a minute to read this checklist – the chances are that it will get you back on the road to success.

☑ A click ALWAYS gets at least one reward.

☑ Click as soon as your dog begins doing the move you want, then reward.

☑ Only use high-value treats and plenty of them (see page 12).

☑ Only click once at any one time, even if you give lots of treats.

☑ Give your dog time to work out for himself what is required.

☑ Build up gradually – at the start of a new trick, click for small steps towards the end goal. For example, to get your dog to twist, you may begin by clicking for just a turn of his head, where he could turn a full circle for a click once he's got the idea.

☑ Keep your dog guessing – about when and how many treats he will get. Although rewards must always be worthwhile, sometimes give a handful for doing particularly well and occasionally ask for two or three repetitions of a move before rewarding.

☑ Don't always click at the end of a behaviour, as this will teach your dog to always stop dead at this point. For example, on circle moves, sometimes click after half a revolution, sometimes after one-and-a-half circles.

☑ You get what you click, so make sure your timing is right.

☑ Experiment! The clicker is very versatile and its advantages are best discovered through trying different things. You can do little harm and any undesirable behaviours that you accidentally train in your dog can usually be just as easily untrained.

Walk this way

THE LESSON

- Dog and owner walking together, side by side, with your dog on a loose lead
- You take your first step towards working your dog off lead

Loose-lead therapy

How a dog walks on his lead can affect how he reacts to different situations. A tight lead can give a bold, aggressive dog more confidence, because he feels you are right behind him, as the pack would be. But this type of dog is often unassertive when on a loose lead. A tight lead can also make a nervous dog more worried, as he senses the tension and feels you are worried, too. With these dogs, a loose lead will make them more confident.

Is this you? When your dog pulls tight on his lead, you are off balance and out of control. To successfully teach your dog tricks, he needs first to be close to you, and second paying attention. A dog that is constantly at the opposite end of the lead to you and looking the other way isn't going to learn much at all. So, put yourself back in charge with this simple exercise. You need to show your dog that it is much more rewarding to stay close to you and that hauling on his lead only results in neck ache.

Most tricks are best taught with your dog off lead, and having your dog walking calmly beside you on a loose lead is the foundation to this. In addition, he'll be a pleasure to exercise and your arms can return to their normal length!

1. When your dog pulls, stop and plant yourself to the floor. Stay where you are and wait for him to stop or turn towards you. As soon as the lead goes slack, click.

2 Immediately walk forwards to meet your dog, so that you come together again with him on your left side.

key points

● Avoid letting your lead hang too low when your dog is walking well, so it cannot trip up either of you.

● With particularly strong dogs, hold the lead with both hands so that it comes from your dog, through your left hand, then diagonally across your body into your right hand. This will give you more control should your dog suddenly pull.

● Working your dog on the outside of a circle will encourage him to watch you, as you are in effect always turning and walking away from him.

3 Once you are side by side with your dog on a loose lead, give him a treat. Repeat the exercise several times – your dog will soon hang back beside your leg in anticipation of another reward.

4 As your dog gets the idea, begin working him in a large circle. At this stage, always have him on the outside of the circle, whether he is on your left or right – he will find it easier to achieve a flowing movement. Walk at a brisk pace for three or four strides, and if he is still on a loose lead and focused on you, click, then stop and reward him. Get his attention back onto your hand before setting off again to repeat the process.

Total recall

THE LESSON

● Dog learns that coming to you whenever you call him is always positive and more worthwhile than anything else he could be doing

There is little point in having a dog who can perform spectacular tricks if you can't get him to come to you when you want. In order to be able to train him or for him to perform, as well as to keep him safe, you need to be able to call your dog to you instantly. For him to leave the exciting things he's just found, your dog needs to be convinced that you're a worthwhile bet. After all, why should he drop what he's doing unless there's something in it for him?

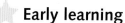

1 Wait until your dog is a little way from you and call him by name to get his attention. If you need to, rustle your treat bag or pot to get him to look towards you. As soon as he turns to face you, click.

⭐ Early learning

Teaching a dog to stay with or come back to you should begin in puppyhood. Many people do not trust their puppies enough to let them off the lead, when in fact this is the time that they are most likely to stick with their human 'pack'. Choose safe, secure places and deliberately walk away from your pup as he watches. His curiosity and need for reassurance will soon get the better of him.

② Your dog should already understand that a click means a treat, so he'll come to you to get his reward. It really is as easy as that.

③ As soon as he comes to you, reward him. If he's a little bit reluctant to come in close, crouch down or even take a step or two backwards. With the exercise complete, walk away a short distance before recalling him again. Once your dog is coming to you quickly and reliably as soon as you call, introduce the command 'come'. Call his name, command him and, as he comes towards you, click. Treat as soon as he reaches you.

Key points

● Call your dog's name only once, so that it maintains impact. Make your voice exciting, backed up with treats or a toy to ensure that you get a reaction. Repeated calling will tell him exactly where you are, so he doesn't even have to raise his head to look. He will also quickly 'tune out'

your voice if you keep shouting but nothing else interesting happens.

● Many dogs won't return to their owners because they are punished when they do finally go back. This just teaches the dog that going to their person is unpleasant.

● Another common cause of a dog not recalling is the owner chasing after him. A dog will think you are playing a great game. If you are struggling to call your dog back and it is safe to do so, get his attention and then run away from him instead. He is likely to quickly follow.

Take a seat

THE LESSON

● Your dog sits on command, whether he is standing or lying down

1 Hold a treat in the underhand position (see page 13) at your dog's nose level and call your dog so that he is standing in front of you at arm's length.

To perform tricks, your dog needs to be agile and able to move between different positions easily, especially if you want him to do a sequence of moves. The basis of many tricks will be a sit, so as well as doing this on command, he needs to be able to move into sit from whatever he was doing before.

Teaching your dog to sit from any position is all about positioning his nose correctly, as this will influence how he moves his hindquarters. If your dog's nose is held high, it is physically easier for him to keep his hindquarters low.

2 In one smooth, steady movement, rotate your hand to the overhand position (see page 13) and raise it straight above your dog's nose, before pushing it out towards your dog's tail. His nose will follow upwards and then tip back slightly, making it easier for him to drop his hindquarters. As soon as he moves into a sit, click. Once he is sitting, give him his reward. Repeat until your dog understands the move, then add in the 'sit' command just before you click.

3 The same principle is used to get your dog to sit from a lying position. First, hold the treat in the underhand position near to his nose.

4 Move your hand steadily upwards so that your dog raises his nose, changing into the overhand position to bring him up to full stretch.

5 Now push your hand steadily upwards and backwards so that, to follow the treat, your dog has to push himself upwards and step backwards with his front legs into a sit. Click just before he reaches the sitting position and reward once he's there.

Key points

● As you move your dog from a down to a sit, make sure he doesn't stand first before sitting. You are aiming for him to hinge upwards in one, smooth move.

● When teaching your dog to sit from a down position, stand up rather than crouch.

● When asked to sit from standing, small dogs often find walking backwards easier. To overcome this habit, break the move down, clicking first for just a slight lift of the nose, again when the head tips back, then again when the hindquarters drop a little, and so on. You can also position your dog where there is a wall behind him, so that backward movement when sitting is limited.

Sitting styles

Did you know that from a standing position dogs can sit in two different ways? Those favouring a 'forwards' sit keep their front legs still and bring their hindlegs under them to meet their front paws. Big breeds and those with a 'stiff-legged' gait, such as Dobermans, Standard Poodles and larger terrier breeds, tend to 'backwards' sit. Keeping their hind feet planted, they draw their front feet back to their hind feet and simply hinge backwards into a sit.

Stand and deliver

THE LESSON
- Whether from sitting or lying, dog moves into a standing position on command
- Help to teach your dog to become 'back-end aware'

Many tricks involving backward movement or standing on the hindlegs require your dog to be able to move easily into the standing position. For a dog to walk backwards or upright, bow and many other things, he needs to be strong in his hindlegs and confident about positioning them.

As you teach your dog to stand promptly on command, aim to get him pushing himself up smartly with his hindlegs, rather than pulling himself into position with his front legs.

Hindleg help

If dogs can judge the position of their hindquarters and place their hindlegs precisely, they will then move equally fluently at both ends of their body. One way to teach them to do this is to get them to move into a stand by 'snapping up' with their hindlegs. When your dog is lying or sitting, bring his food bowl to him and put it on the floor right under his chin, between his front legs. He will then 'flick' his hindlegs up and move into a stand to be able to reach it.

Stand from sit

1 To teach your dog to stand from sitting, begin with a treat held in the underhand position (see page 13) level with his nose.

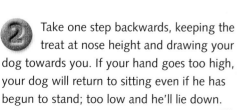

2 Take one step backwards, keeping the treat at nose height and drawing your dog towards you. If your hand goes too high, your dog will return to sitting even if he has begun to stand; too low and he'll lie down.

3 As your dog squares up into a stand, click and then treat. Practise this until your dog gets the idea and then add in the command 'stand' just before you click.

Stand from down

1 From the down position, move your dog into a standing position by first holding a treat in the underhand position (see page 13) near his nose.

2 As before, take a step backwards, but this time move your hand diagonally upwards to bring your dog's nose up. His hindlegs will follow, and as he reaches standing, click and treat. Again, as he begins to get the idea add the command 'stand' just before you click.

Down time

To do tricks such as roll over (see page 54) or play dead (see page 56), your dog needs go into the down position quickly and easily with a clean drop to the floor. This needs forethought, clear communication and trust to be successful as you are asking him to go into a vulnerable position.

Down from stand

1   With your dog standing, hold a treat close to his nose in the underhand position (see page 13).

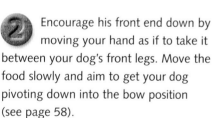

2   Encourage his front end down by moving your hand as if to take it between your dog's front legs. Move the food slowly and aim to get your dog pivoting down into the bow position (see page 58).

3   Keep your hand low and still and your dog's hindquarters should drop, as lying is a more comfortable position for him. When he is almost in the down, click then reward once he is down. Repeat this until your dog goes down confidently. Then add the verbal command 'down' and practise – your dog will soon learn to drop on the verbal command alone.

The three downs

There are three different down positions. The 'upright' down (left) is what you are aiming for when your dog needs to move quickly between positions. When your dog is relaxed, he may lie on one hip so that his front end is still upright but his feet are to one side of his body (middle). Then there is the 'flat' down, used for roll overs (see page 54) and playing dead (see page 56), where he lies stretched out on one side of his body (right).

Down from sit

1 From a sitting position, move your dog into the down position by luring him forwards and downwards. Aim to move his front legs only, leaving enough room for them both to come straight forwards.

2 When he cannot reach forwards any further without moving his hindlegs, move the treat down to the floor. As he sinks into a down, click and reward. Practise, then add the 'down' command.

Hold it!

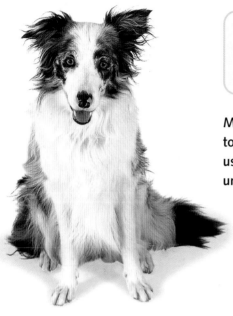

THE LESSON

● On the command 'wait', dog remains in whatever position he is in, until you release him

Many tricks require your dog to stay in a single position, so you need to be able to tell him to 'hold it right there'. The 'wait' command is used to do this, telling your dog to keep whatever position he is in until you say he can move or you give the next command.

Teach the wait in simple positions first, such as the sit, down and stand, and once your dog understands, you can use it for begging (see page 42), playing dead (see page 56) or anything else that takes your fancy.

1 Begin by recalling your dog close to you and commanding him to 'sit'. However, instead of clicking as he sits, wait two or three seconds with him in a sit, then click and treat. Now command 'sit' again and this time don't click for five or six seconds. This will teach him to be patient for his reward and that receiving a treat does not necessarily signal the end of the exercise. Once the dog has succeeded several times, introduce the 'wait' command by saying 'sit, wait'.

2 Once your dog understands the basic idea, command him to 'sit, wait', but this time take a step backwards, away from him. If he remains sitting, click and go back to him to reward.

Key points

● If your dog breaks from a position as you click, but before you give the treat, simply put him back where you had told him to wait and then treat. There is no need to click again, as you are still finishing the previous click/treat combination.

● The giving of the treat should not become the cue to end any exercise, especially the wait. Prevent this by giving a variable number of treats so that your dog remains focused on you in case there is more food coming.

● Use a release word such as 'OK', which indicates to your dog that the wait exercise has finished and he is now allowed to leave his spot.

● As you initially move around your dog while he waits, take care to keep your hands still and your movement controlled. Waving arms can be confusing, appearing as signals, while fast moves may look like an invitation to come and play.

Square standing

Make it easier for your dog to wait in the standing position by making sure he is comfortable. Teach him to stand squarely with a 'leg at each corner'. Use a treat to shuffle him forwards and backwards until he is standing with his front paws in line and back paws well under him and in line, then click and treat. Practise this so that it becomes second nature to him. Gradually he will learn to take up this stance on his own.

3 Build up the distance you can move away from him by taking another step backwards with each repetition of the exercise. Once your dog is happy for you to move away some distance, try moving from side to side. Always click when you are at the furthest point away and return to your dog to reward him.

4 Now try linking the 'wait' command to other positions, such as the sit or stand. Give the position command first and then add 'wait'. Begin close to your dog and build up the distance.

Positions please

THE LESSON

- Dog and owner begin by facing each other
- Dog moves in a loop behind the owner to finish standing straight beside his owner's leg, so that both dog and owner are now facing in the same direction
- Dog enhances his 'back-end awareness'

By teaching your dog a good heel position while walking, you'll open up the possibilities of what he can do at faster paces or, for example, on his hind legs or crawling. Moves look much slicker too if you are working close together, in harmony.

Aim to teach your dog to position himself tightly beside your leg, with his body straight. However, it is also the way your dog moves to your heel that is important. By teaching him to loop behind you to get into the heel position, he is learning to step well with his hind legs and to swing his quarters separately to his front end. This is vital for backwards moves, such as reversing around you.

1 Start with your dog facing you, slightly over to your left side. Stand with your feet together and hold a treat at nose level, close to your dog.

2 With your right foot planted, take your left foot straight back one step and lure your dog away from your body to the left and slightly behind you.

● Always start this exercise with your dog in front of you, as it is then easier to make the loop correctly.

● Do not turn your dog in a loop away from your body – he should always turn towards you, reinforcing the idea that he should keep looking to you.

● Once you have practised this move a number of times and taught your dog the 'close' command, try simply holding the treat close to your leg in the position where you want his nose to end up and then giving the command. You should find that your dog will swing his hindquarters around and position himself straight and close beside you.

● Don't forget to practise this move on both sides of your body.

● Make sure you give your dog enough room to turn completely before coming back to your side.

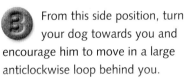 From this side position, turn your dog towards you and encourage him to move in a large anticlockwise loop behind you.

4 Make the arc big enough for your dog to turn 180 degrees so that his nose comes round just behind your left leg. You are aiming for him to then step his hindlegs to the right, to bring them in line with his head. As soon as he steps round with his hind feet, click.

5 Step forward with your left leg to bring your feet together again and your dog forwards in line with your leg. Once your dog is standing close beside you with his body straight, click and give him a treat. Repeat the move by simply turning to face your dog and then following these steps again. Add the command 'close' just prior to clicking.

Shaping up

It's time to test if your dog is focusing on you and clued in fully to all you have taught him so far. Put his lead away and get active with some heelwork in different directions, on different sides of your body and in varying patterns. Wherever you go, your dog should remain in position and attentive.

As well as keeping him focused, working him to heel in different ways will improve his flexibility and the strength in his hindquarters. Always start with the side he finds easiest first and keep the shapes large. As your dog becomes more supple, you can ask for tighter turns.

Circling with your dog on the outside
Practise large circles with your dog on your outside. Go clockwise when he's on your left and anticlockwise when he's on your right. Move at a brisk pace to maintain your dog's interest and momentum. Hold your treats in a position that allows your dog's head and neck to be comfortable and doesn't force his hindquarters to swing out. Circling naturally turns your dog towards you and encourages him to stride out to keep up with you.

⭐ Teaching the trot

Dogs naturally pace (move the two legs on one side of the body and then the two on the opposite side) to conserve energy, so if you see your dog pacing, you know he may not be giving his all. Circle work is good for teaching your dog to trot (when diagonal pairs of legs move together) instead. Encourage your dog actively forwards on the outside of a circle and he is likely to change from pacing to trotting. This will help him become more balanced, alert and energetic for training.

🐾 Key points

● Always begin circle work by asking for just a few good steps at heel from your dog, clicking while he is still moving well. Then ask him to stop a step or two later to give him his treat, as a dog cannot eat and maintain a good heel position at the same time.

● When starting a figure-of-eight, always begin with the circle where your dog is on the outside.

Circling with your dog on the inside

Now try circling anticlockwise with your dog on your left and vice versa. Keep to big circles initially so that your dog doesn't have to turn away from you too much and lose momentum. If your dog is able to work fluently on the inside of a circle, he is becoming 'back-end aware'.

Figure-of-eights

Next practise your heelwork with two circles joined to form a figure-of-eight. Your dog will need to adapt from being on the outside to the inside of the circle and back again. Try to walk the circle with your dog on the outside slightly faster than the one with him on the inside. A figure-of-eight can also help a dog who finds being on the inside tricky – you can use the straight steps as you cross over to get him back into a good heel position and rebalanced.

How do you do

THE TRICK
- ● Dog learns to 'give paw' on command to shake hands with you
- ● Develop the move to become marching

This trick is quick and easy to teach, especially if your dog naturally uses his paws rather than his mouth to try to get hold of things. As well as being a cute trick in itself, the 'give paw' command forms the basis of other tricks, including waving (see page 38), marching (see box opposite) and high fives (see page 44).

Although on most occasions dogs need to know that they should not snatch food from your hand during training, it is sometimes helpful to use this natural response to teach new behaviours. A dog who knows you are holding food in a closed hand will usually try to get it with his mouth and paw. These movements can then be developed into tricks. However, to avoid confusing your dog, use a verbal cue such as 'get it', which indicates that he is allowed to try to get the food.

① With your dog sitting, kneel down to face him, sitting back on your heels. Hold a treat firmly in your hand so that your dog is able to smell it but not get it. Position your hand near his nose but to one side of his body so that he turns his head slightly. This will take the weight off the leg he is facing away from. Encourage him to try to get the treat – most dogs will try to open your hand with their paw. As soon as his paw touches your hand, click, open your hand and reward. Repeat this several times with both front paws. Then add in a verbal command just before you click, such as 'touch' for the right leg and 'tap' for the left.

2 With a treat in one hand, hold out your other hand in an open position towards the leg you want your dog to lift. As soon as your dog touches your open hand with his paw, click and reward from your other hand. Repeat several times with both front legs.

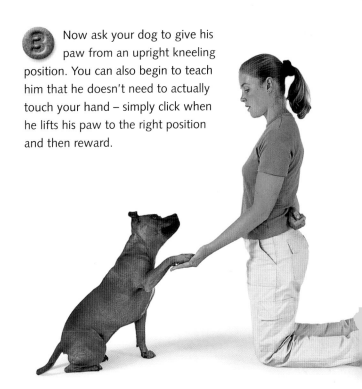

3 Now ask your dog to give his paw from an upright kneeling position. You can also begin to teach him that he doesn't need to actually touch your hand – simply click when he lifts his paw to the right position and then reward.

Key points

● If your dog is not keen to lift his paw himself, pick up his foot with your clicker hand. With the paw raised, click and give him a treat from your other hand.

● Repeat this a few times and your dog should begin to associate lifting his paw with getting a reward. You can then try Step 1 again.

4 Keep practising and you'll soon be able to get your dog to say 'how do you do' with either paw from a sitting position simply by showing an open hand on the side you wish him to give his paw.

On the march

Develop the trick into your dog standing and marching with his front legs, simply by asking for each foot in turn. Start slowly and build up the number of steps as your dog gets confident with the move. You can even march in unison by teaching him to lift his paw as you lift your foot. Simply lift your feet as you give the hand signals – with practice, your dog will link the foot signals to the moves and you will be able to drop the hand signals completely.

Making waves

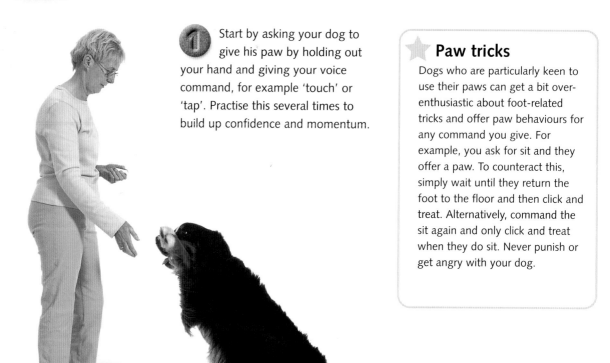

THE TRICK

● Dog moves his paw up and down to wave a warm welcome or a fond farewell

To get your dog to perform a proper wave, you simply need to refine what he does to give a paw (see page 36). The paw lift is the same – you now just need to introduce movement and encourage your dog to repeat the pattern to produce the full effect. The waving action is created by your dog learning to give his paw at several different heights.

1 Start by asking your dog to give his paw by holding out your hand and giving your voice command, for example 'touch' or 'tap'. Practise this several times to build up confidence and momentum.

⭐ Paw tricks

Dogs who are particularly keen to use their paws can get a bit over-enthusiastic about foot-related tricks and offer paw behaviours for any command you give. For example, you ask for sit and they offer a paw. To counteract this, simply wait until they return the foot to the floor and then click and treat. Alternatively, command the sit again and only click and treat when they do sit. Never punish or get angry with your dog.

② This time, as your dog lifts his paw and starts to stretch towards you, move your hand up, just out of his reach. He is likely to reach out further to try to make contact with you. As his paw reaches a more extended position, click and treat. Repeat this several times, each time clicking when his paw is at a different height.

The dog goes as if to shake hands…

…but continues to lift his paw…

…and strikes out upwards before repeating the move again to create a wave.

③ Gradually delay the click so that your dog has to stretch out for your hand once and then do another lower paw lift before you click and reward. Then wait for him to reach out twice before clicking and so on. Introduce the verbal command 'wave' at the end of the sequence of 'give paw' commands, for example, 'tap, tap, wave', then click and treat. As he develops a waving motion, like the sequence above, you can start to drop the command you use for giving a paw and just use 'wave'.

Shake a leg

Most dogs can quickly be taught to lift a front paw on command, but how about lifting a hindleg on cue? This trick can then be developed into a stretch, a back leg march or even as a pretend cocked leg! It is great for further increasing your dog's awareness of his hindquarters because he has to move his back legs independently. It is also a useful skill in a daily domestic situation, as you can get your dog to lift his feet on command when you want to clean or check them after walks.

 Hindleg marching

Once you have taught your dog to lift both hind paws, you can develop this trick into hindleg marching using similar steps to those used for training front leg marching (see page 37). Alternate your left- and right-leg verbal commands, and once your dog has lifted one leg and then the other, click and treat. Gradually extend the sequence by progressively adding a few more steps before clicking and rewarding. You can then teach your dog to lift his back paw when you raise your leg backwards by giving the verbal cue and moving your leg at the same time. After that, you will be ready for some really fancy footwork!

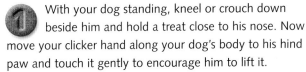

1 With your dog standing, kneel or crouch down beside him and hold a treat close to his nose. Now move your clicker hand along your dog's body to his hind paw and touch it gently to encourage him to lift it.

2 Most dogs have quite sensitive feet, so a gentle touch will usually cause them to move their paws. As soon as your dog lifts his paw, click and give him a treat. Repeat this several times so that your dog understands what you want him to do. Then add in the verbal command, such as 'foot', just before you click.

3 Practise the trick, giving your dog the verbal cue and slowly withdrawing the touch on his foot. As he gets the idea, you can try standing up and just giving the verbal command. Then, if you wish, follow the steps through again and teach your dog to raise his other hind paw on a different verbal command.

Key points

● If your dog isn't keen to raise his paw, try tickling between his toes. Many dogs are super-sensitive in this area and will quickly snatch their foot up.

● If your dog still isn't persuaded to lift his paw, pick it up with your hand and then click and treat. Repeat this a few times and he should then understand what you are asking for.

● If you choose to teach this trick for both hind paws, choose verbal commands that are distinct and memorable so that you don't confuse yourself and your dog. Try choosing words that relate to your dog's paw colours or markings.

Say please

> **THE TRICK**
> ● Dog lifts up both front paws and sits back and balances on his haunches

Dogs and begging go hand in hand, but, in reality, few pets can actually perform this trick. Your dog needs to learn to balance in a more upright position and this skill will form the foundation of other tricks such as high fives (see page 44) and walking on his hindlegs (see page 48).

Don't forget that this trick should be taught only to dogs over six months old in order to avoid placing undue strain on developing hip joints. Even with adult dogs, don't be tempted to relentlessly repeat the more upright tricks and avoid asking for too much too soon.

1 Begin with your dog sitting in front of you, leaving enough space between you for him to raise his front paws off the ground.

2 Holding a treat to your dog's nose, move your hand upwards and push it away from you so that your dog tilts his head backwards. This will encourage him to take his front paws off the ground. As soon as both paws leave the floor, click.

⭐ Giving support

Younger dogs and big breeds tend to find it hard to balance in the beg position, so help them initially by supporting a paw – lift their foot and then take the treat over their head to encourage the other paw to follow.

Alternatively, they may choose to hold onto your wrist with both paws. This is fine to begin with, but will eventually need to be phased out. Do this by holding the treat in an overhand position (see page 13) with your arm arched up out of reach.

● If your dog keeps pushing up with his hindlegs into an upright stand, you are asking him to raise his paws too high. Ask for a bit less and click earlier.

● Experiment using an underhand and overhand position (see page 13) to see what works best for you. Underhand positions are often better for younger dogs.

● If your dog tips his head back but doesn't leave the floor, try your 'give paw' command (see page 36) to help him get the idea.

● With tricks like the beg, where you work particularly close to your dog's head, consider using a quieter clicker so you don't hurt his sensitive ears. Alternatively, hold the clicker further away from him or muffle it in a pocket.

● Small dogs usually find it very easy to push up out of a sit and onto their back legs, so they can be tricky to keep on their haunches. Take care not to move the treat very far from their nose, and if necessary, lay your hand on their hindquarters to help discourage them from springing up.

3 Your dog is likely to return his feet to the floor until he gets more balanced – let him do what is comfortable and reward him.

4 Repeat the exercise, each time asking your dog to lift his paws a little bit higher to enable him to find his point of balance. Initially click when your dog has held a position just for a second or two before rewarding. Once your dog can lift his paws and sit back on his haunches fluently, add in a verbal command such as 'both' or 'beg'.

High five!

Celebrate your canine successes in style by teaching your dog a cool high five. This paw-to-hand connection clearly demonstrates a strong dog-and-owner partnership and is bound to bring you a welcome feel-good factor. If your dog can already give a paw (see page 36) and beg (see page 42), this is a straight-forward yet impressive trick to teach.

 With your dog sitting, get down to his level and give your command for 'give paw' (see page 36) while offering your open hand. Click as he touches your hand and reward. Repeat this a few times to build your dog's confidence and momentum in the way he is working.

2 Now change to a raised high-five hand and again tell him to 'give paw'. Most dogs have little difficulty transferring the command to this different hand position. As soon as he touches your raised hand, click and treat. Repeat this several times before offering your raised hand, while saying 'high five' as your dog makes contact with you. Click and reward. Practise this so that your dog will happily do the move cued from the 'high five' verbal command.

3 Now practise with the other front paw in the same way until your dog is just as fluently tapping your raised hand on this side when you give the 'high five' verbal command.

4 Now stand up and get your dog into the beg position.

5 With both hands in the raised position command 'high five'. If your dog goes to touch both hands at the same time, click and reward. If your dog misses one hand, change your position to improve your dog's chances of making contact with both hands and try again. Continue practising until perfect.

Stand tall

For some dogs, especially small ones, standing on their hindlegs appears to be second nature, while others find this position hard. Bigger breeds in particular can find this move a challenge. But all dogs are different, so have a go and see whether your dog develops a taste for standing tall.

Before you get started, take a good look at your dog to see if his type and build will help or hinder him. Also consider your dog's age. Dogs under 12 months old should not be asked to stand upright and older dogs should have their health and fitness taken into account.

Before you start learning this trick, make sure your dog can readily give a paw on command (see page 36) and warm up by practising this a few times.

1 Hold a treat in the overhand position (see page 13) and get your dog standing in front of you. Stand or kneel, depending on the size of your dog.

⭐ Hindleg habits

You should already have a good idea of whether your dog is likely to take to tricks involving him being up on his hindlegs. Many dogs will stand upright of their own accord in order to see things better. For example, they may stand up with their front paws against a tree to look for that elusive cat or squirrel, or stand upright unaided to look over long grass or to find out what's in the food bowl you are carrying. Next time you give your dog his food, raise his bowl out of view and see how he reacts.

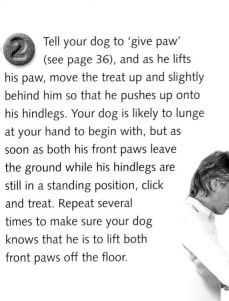

2 Tell your dog to 'give paw' (see page 36), and as he lifts his paw, move the treat up and slightly behind him so that he pushes up onto his hindlegs. Your dog is likely to lunge at your hand to begin with, but as soon as both his front paws leave the ground while his hindlegs are still in a standing position, click and treat. Repeat several times to make sure your dog knows that he is to lift both front paws off the floor.

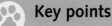

Key points

● Consider your dog's size, type, age and health before working on a trick that involves standing on his hindlegs.

● Although the command 'both' may also be used for a beg (see page 42), the dog will still understand the move required by the context in which it is presented. To the dog, 'both' means raise both front paws off the ground – he will simply do this from a sit (to produce a beg) or from a stand (to stand upright), as asked.

● Many dogs will find standing still when in an upright position harder than moving slightly, especially to begin with.

3 Gradually work on increasing the height that your dog lifts his paws and improving his balance. Then add in a command for standing upright, such as 'both'. With practice, aim to achieve a good balanced standing position for a second or two before clicking and treating.

4 If you have a small dog, wait until he is confident with the move before commanding him from a standing position yourself. Often little dogs can feel overpowered by an owner leaning over them and will consequently become reluctant to respond to the command.

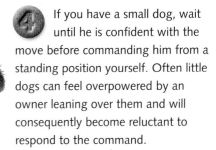

Walk tall

If your dog has already learned to stand on his hindlegs (see page 46), he should be able to take some steps, too. However, don't necessarily expect your dog to walk as you would – many dogs find walking backwards easier by stepping with one foot then bringing the other paw to meet the first, so producing a slightly lop-sided gait.

Try teaching your dog to go backwards first, and if he takes it all in his stride, have a go at forwards and sideways moves in addition. You can then try altering your position so that you and your dog walk side by side, for example, instead of facing each other.

1 Get a particularly high-value treat or favourite toy and then ask your dog to stand on his hindlegs.

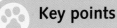

Key points

● Make sure you click when your dog is actually stepping – then he will associate the reward with the movement and it will be easier for him to learn that the action is continuous.

● For moves on the hindlegs, keep practice sessions short. These tricks require concentration, strength and balance, and your dog is likely to tire easily. A tired dog is unlikely to enjoy himself.

● To teach your dog to walk forwards, follow the same process, but stay beside rather than in front of him. Encourage small steps by holding a toy or treat above him and slightly ahead. By facing him and walking backwards with a lure he is more likely to lunge forwards and overbalance.

② Hold the treat high and walk towards your dog. To keep the toy in view, your dog will have to take a step backwards. As soon as he moves a back paw, click and reward him. Then get him balanced in the upright stand and repeat the exercise again.

 As he learns to balance, ask for a second step before clicking and rewarding. Build this up gradually in order to teach your dog to walk backwards as you walk towards him. Add in the command 'back' just before clicking so that your dog links this to the movement. As your dog increases in strength, agility and confidence, he will begin to take larger steps backwards and increase in speed.

Knowing your dog's limitations

Walking on the hindlegs can be taught with the owner supporting the dog to help him balance. However, this approach doesn't allow you to judge if your dog is physically capable of doing this difficult move by himself, or willing to do it. In either case, the dog is unlikely ever to be able to perform the trick alone, so it is better to concentrate on moves he is more able to achieve. Trying to produce a difficult trick with an unwilling or unsuited dog only results in frustration and upset for both dog and owner.

A high five on high

If you've already taught your dog the basic high five (see page 44) and he is able to balance well on his hindlegs (see page 46), this trick should soon fall into place. Ideally, your dog should be working well on the verbal commands, without a lure.

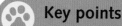

Key points

- Don't hold a clicker in your hand for this trick, as a folded hand will confuse your dog. Enlist the help of a friend, use a button clicker (see page 10) or use a verbal signal such as 'yes' instead of a click.

- If your dog puts both his paws onto one of you hands, wait until he separates them before clicking.

- If your dog is struggling to do the high five, go back a few steps and practise it again with him in the sitting position (see page 44).

 Face your dog and give your command for standing on his hindlegs (see page 46).

2 Now give your 'high five' command (see page 44) as you show the palms of both your hands. Your dog should reach up and touch his paws to your hands. As soon as he makes contact with one, as long as the other paw is close to your other hand, click and reward. Now practise until he can hit a hand with each paw every time.

Doing the twist

THE TRICK

● Dog stands on his hindlegs and twists on the spot with stretched front paws to perform a pirouette on command

 Key points

● Use your right hand for a clockwise twist and the left for an anticlockwise twist, so your dog will know the right direction by the arm you use and can move forwards freely into the twist. If you get confused think about swimming the breaststroke!

● Give your dog plenty of room to learn to twist, so he is not afraid of knocking against anything.

● Teach your dog to twist the way he finds easiest first.

This trick looks great when the dog is moving fluently and confidently, so take the time to practise and increase the level of difficulty gradually. Rushing the early stages will only produce a stilted move or hesitant dog.

1 Stand or kneel in front of your dog and ask him to stand on his hindlegs. Hold a treat in the overhand position (see page 13) centrally above your dog. Using just your wrist, move the treat slowly in a circular motion so that your dog has to turn his head to watch it.

2 Keep moving the treat in a circular motion so that the dog's body will have to follow his head movement, and he will take a step. Click as soon as he moves a hind foot and reward.

3 Continue in the same way to complete the circle in small steps. As your dog gets the idea, build up the number of steps he has to do before he is clicked and rewarded and add in the verbal command 'twist'. Once he has achieved a 360-degree twist on a single click, withhold the click until one-and-a-half turns, then two turns and so on to create a continuous pirouette.

Get the low down

This trick can be developed in many fun ways, for example your dog creeping up behind you. But to get your dog to do it well will be a test of your skills. The correct positioning of the lure is crucial and requires you to be able to understand the effect of even tiny movements of your hand on your dog's body posture.

Crawling requires your dog to be very agile and supple, so make sure your dog is physically up to the trick. Also, teach this before the roll over (see page 54) or you could find that your dog spends more time with his legs in the air than creeping along the ground.

1 Introduce your dog to the idea of crawling by sitting on the floor with your knees raised and your dog in an upright down (see page 28) at right angles to you. Hold a treat in the hand on the opposite side to your dog and lure him through the tunnel created by your legs while repeating the command 'down'. Click as he is moving under your legs and reward him as he emerges. Practise this several times.

2 With your dog in an upright down, face him and hold a treat to his nose. Aim to keep his nose approximately 5–7.5 cm (2–3 in) off the floor and his head straight.

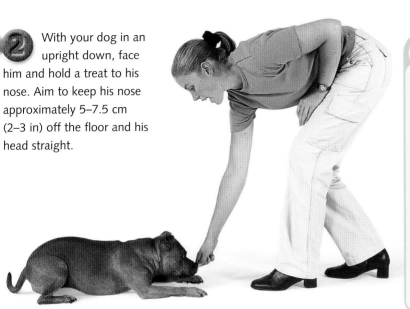

Key points

● Big dogs may be unable to crawl fully, but will creep along with their front end on the ground while they walk with their hindquarters raised.

● If your dog suffers from any joint problems, he is unlikely to be able to do this trick – instead, look for other tricks more suited to his abilities.

● If your dog seems reluctant to crawl, check the type of surface that you are asking him to move along – cold, rough or slippery surfaces will be off-putting.

3 Move the food steadily away from him, while repeating the 'down' command, but no more than 15 cm (6 in). As soon as your dog edges forwards, while remaining low, click and treat. Practise this, and as he gets the idea, add the command 'crawl' or 'creep' with your repeated 'down' commands, for example, 'down, down, down, crawl', click and treat.

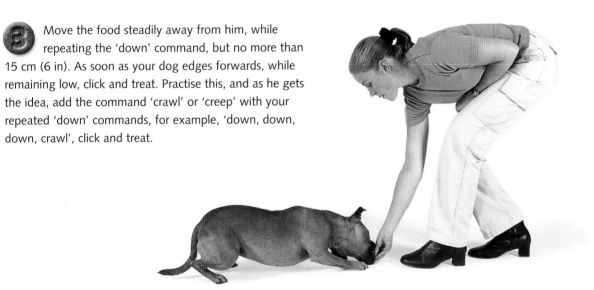

A lesson in luring

The position and movement of the lure is vital for this trick, as this determines how your dog moves his body. A treat held too low will cause your dog to tuck his paws in, twist his head and raise his hindquarters. Moving his reward too fast will cause him to leap up, while too slow will cause frustration because he isn't getting it and doesn't understand what you want as he is receiving no direction.

4 Build up the distance your dog crawls by clicking and treating after two shuffles forward, then three and so on. Once he understands the move and can crawl some distance, cut out the 'down' commands. When he can be cued just from the word 'crawl', try standing or moving yourself to develop the trick.

On a roll

THE TRICK

● Dog starts in an upright down, rolls over on his back and returns to an upright down on command

This move will form the basis of the 'play dead' trick on page 56, so it's worth taking the time to get it really fluent. Before you start consider the floor surface you are asking your dog to roll over. It should be comfortable for him so he isn't put off doing the trick.

Most dogs learn this move quite easily and may get over-enthusiastic about it, offering roll overs at any opportunity. Once your dog has got the idea, limit the rehearsals and keep this trick interspersed with others.

1 Kneel down and position your dog in an upright down (see page 28) in front of you. Hold a treat close to your dog's nose in the underhand position (see page 13).

2 Turn your dog's nose towards his shoulder by moving into the overhand position and arching your arm over his head. If you are rolling your dog onto his left side, use your right hand. Keep moving your dog's nose around and upwards towards the point of his shoulders. Gradually he will become unbalanced.

3 Eventually your dog will reach a point where it is easier for him to flop onto his side, into a flat down (see page 29). Click as he rolls flat and reward him when his head is on the floor.

(see page 29)

4 Now repeat the luring pattern above, again moving your hand in a clockwise circle to turn your dog's head towards his side and then up to his shoulder. This time the movement of his head will cause his hindlegs to follow, so he will roll over onto his other side. As soon as his body begins to flip over onto the other side, click. Once he is lying flat, treat.

5 Encourage your dog into an upright down by holding a treat at nose level and moving towards his feet. As he comes up, bring the food towards you. Practise several times before trying to do the roll over in one flowing move, without stopping in the flat positions. In time, add the 'roll over' command before clicking and treating.

Key points

● Make sure you have the correct hand luring your dog or you could end up in a knot with a rather confused dog!

● Aim to click as your dog rolls but when he is past the point of return. That way you reward the actual movement and it's inevitable that he is going to achieve the full move.

● If your dog finds rolling from the flat down on one side to his other side difficult, help him initially by lifting his front paw nearest the floor.

Building confidence

Your dog needs to be happy to go into a down before trying any of these more advanced 'floor' moves. A dog that is reluctant to lie down on command is likely to lack confidence and feel vulnerable, and needs to build more trust with his handler. Practise in a relaxed, quiet and comfortable environment with the aim of making the moves fun and easy. Remember that there are no 'wrongs' with clicker training – every lesson should be positive. When working on the roll over, practise Steps 1–3 thoroughly with a more nervous dog before attempting to achieve the full move back to the starting position.

Dead cool

This trick can look spectacular, but needs the dog to drop instantly to the floor and to stay there without a flicker to achieve the full effect. You can make this move as detailed as you wish, teaching your dog to cue from a 'gun' hand signal or even a toy pop gun, stick his legs in the air and even close his eyes!

Before getting stuck in, be sure that your dog can down (see page 28), wait (see page 30) and roll over (see page 54) well. Elements of all these moves are needed for 'play dead'.

1 Ask your dog to 'roll over', and once he is halfway, command him to 'wait'. As soon as he stops where he is, click and treat. Practise this and gradually extend the amount of time you ask him to wait before clicking and rewarding.

2 If you want to teach your dog to hold his paws upwards or outwards, ask him to give his paw (page 36) and offer your hand for him to touch. Click as his leg reaches the point you want and reward. Work up gradually so that your dog learns to hold this leg position.

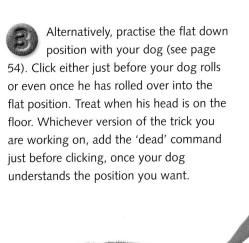

3 Alternatively, practise the flat down position with your dog (see page 54). Click either just before your dog rolls or even once he has rolled over into the flat position. Treat when his head is on the floor. Whichever version of the trick you are working on, add the 'dead' command just before clicking, once your dog understands the position you want.

4 You can then begin to cue the trick from a standing position using the 'dead' command. Once your dog is happily working from this, introduce the visual hand signal of a gun or an actual toy gun…

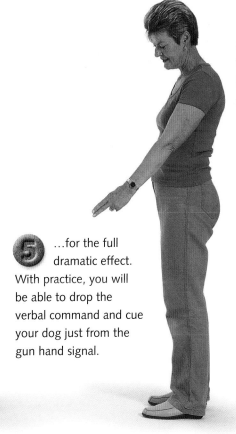

5 …for the full dramatic effect. With practice, you will be able to drop the verbal command and cue your dog just from the gun hand signal.

Take a bow

All good performers know how to encourage and acknowledge audience appreciation at the end of a successful show. Make sure you and your dog finish your tricks in style with a bow. You can develop this to become a bow to one another, or a simultaneous bow to your audience.

To create a good bow, you're aiming for your dog to move as if he is going into a down, but then holding the position just before his hindquarters sink to the floor.

Key points

● Timing is critical – you must click for the drop of the forequarters before your dog is fully committed to going into a down. If you click once he is past the point of return, he will mistakenly think you are rewarding a down.

● This move needs your dog to be supple through his back, so work up gradually to ensure that he is physically capable.

● Although 'bow' may seem the obvious command to use for this move, consider whether your dog may become confused, as the word 'bow' sounds very similar to the 'down' command.

● If your dog insists on going all the way into a down, break the trick into small steps. Work on just tiny moves of the head and neck first, clicking for a dip of the nose, then lowering the head and so on.

1 With your dog standing in front of you, hold a treat to his nose in the underhand position (see page 13).

2 Move the food steadily towards your dog and downwards at a 45-degree angle, as if pushing it between his front legs. Aim to tip his nose downwards and backwards, encouraging him to dip his forequarters. As soon as he does hinge backwards and drop, even slightly, click and treat before he drops into a down.

3 Build up the move by withholding the click a little more each time so that your dog keeps dropping a little lower. In time he will drop down onto his elbows while keeping his hindlegs raised. Once your dog can do this, add in the command such as 'bow', 'bend' or 'stretch' before you click and treat. Practise so that the command is linked to the move.

4 Now try the trick with you kneeling and then standing. If your dog can produce the move from just the verbal command, you can then try turning face-to-face and bowing to each other or even bowing side-by-side to your audience.

Hide your eyes

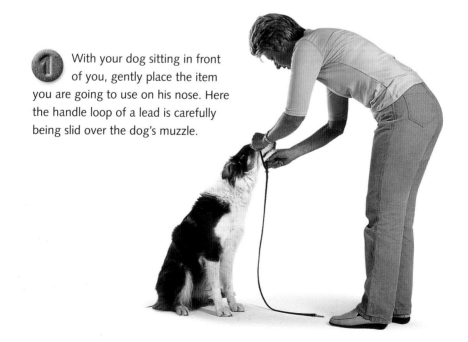

THE TRICK

- Dog puts one or both front paws across his nose, as if hiding his face

This trick is based upon the natural behaviour performed by a dog when he cleans his face. It can be shaped to alter the paw position, or even so that both front paws are used.

To get the basic behaviour, you need to find a trigger for your dog to perform this natural move. Some dogs are quite sensitive around their face and whiskers, so a light touch may be enough. Others may need a little more encouragement, such as a small sticky note stuck onto their fur that will brush off or something carefully looped over their nose. Only use items that will come off easily and not hurt or scare your dog or restrict his breathing.

1 With your dog sitting in front of you, gently place the item you are going to use on his nose. Here the handle loop of a lead is carefully being slid over the dog's muzzle.

2 Command your dog to 'wait' (see page 30) and slowly take your hands away from his face so that you can get your treat and clicker ready. Then give him your release command, allowing him to try to remove the item you have placed on his nose.

(see page 30)

Key points

● If your dog finds this move tricky, try teaching it from the down position (see page 28). Your dog's paws are then closer to his nose and for some dogs this can be easier.

● Once your dog confidently covers his face on command, you can combine this with other moves, for example, in the beg (see page 42) or the bow (see page 58), to produce some fun and effective sequences.

3 As soon as he lifts his paw to brush the item away, click and reward him. Continue to click for each wipe of the paw until the item is removed. Repeat, until your dog understands the movement you want and then add in the verbal command such as 'wipe' or 'face' before you click. Practise until your dog produces the move from the verbal cue alone. Build up the time your dog holds his paw in position by withholding the click or commanding him to 'wait'.

The two-paw hide

To teach your dog to raise both paws to his nose at the same time, place him in a down. Then gently wipe a little bit of soft food onto each side of his muzzle. Allow him to try and rub this off, clicking as soon as he raises either paw to his face and rewarding. Once he has the idea, add in a different verbal command to that used for a single paw, such as 'hide'.

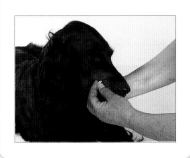

Solo catch

THE TRICK

● Dog balances item on nose before flipping it in the air to catch it

This is quite a traditional trick, but surprisingly difficult to teach. Your dog needs to have good eye-to-mouth coordination, which will only come with practice. Ideally, teach your dog the 'wait' command first (see page 30) so that he will stay still as you place the item on his nose and then wait for your signal.

Although the trick can be taught with a treat, it can be more effective to use a flat object such as a plastic lid or small mat. This prevents your dog snatching treats when he hasn't completed the move and therefore rewarding himself prematurely. Using food to teach the trick can also encourage your dog into short cuts, such as letting the treat conveniently slide off his nose!

1 First, teach your dog to catch. Stand a few steps in front of him, get his attention and then throw a toy or treat for him to catch. If he succeeds, click and treat. If he misses, throw again. Throw accurately and keep practising until your dog is catching more than missing. Then introduce the command 'catch'.

⭐ Catching

Some dogs can be a little lazy about catching and need a bit of motivation. As you teach your dog to catch, try to always get the treat or toy yourself first, if he misses it. This prevents him from getting 'freebies' and rewards when he hasn't achieved the behaviour you are aiming for and adds an element of competition. This can be taken further if you have another dog – the 'catching' dog will become much keener and more focused if he thinks his canine pal is going to get the reward if he misses!

🐾 Key points

● Flatter items tend to be easier for your dog to balance, flip and catch. Make sure they are not too heavy.

● Choose an object that is big enough for your dog to see. Bigger items also tend to stay a little longer in the air. However, if they are too big, your dog won't be able to see round them, so will either refuse to keep them on his nose or be forced to dip his head to see you.

● When balancing the item, encourage your dog to keep his nose level – don't stand over him so that he has to look up to see you.

2 Place your dog in a sit and command him to wait (see page 30). Gently but firmly place the item on his nose, positioning it carefully so that it balances and doesn't interfere with his eyes. Command 'wait' again. After a second or two, click and return to him. Remove the item and give him a treat.

3 Balance the item on your dog's nose and try to encourage him to flip it up. With your dog watching, make a sharp throwing gesture and command 'catch'. You are aiming for your dog to jerk his nose up enough to dislodge the item. Click and reward.

4 Keep practising until your dog achieves a catch, then click and reward. If your dog doesn't get the idea, throw him a few toys or treats to catch before balancing one on his nose again. With practice, he will make the connection.

Face to face

THE TRICK

● Whichever way the owner turns, the dog always faces him or her

As well as tricks that are complete within themselves, you can teach your dog moves that, when put together, can become more of a dance routine, like those seen in the competitive discipline of heelwork to music (see page 124). This is great fun and good for keeping you and your dog fit and agile.

To be able to move well together, your dog needs to learn to look at you for the next signal, but without being as close as you would ask for in obedience training, as you both need to be able to move freely. The 'in front' command is great as a starting point or within a sequence, as it focuses your dog while keeping him moving.

⭐ Working on the hard side

Watch to see from which direction of approach your dog tends to achieve a straighter body position, as all dogs will have an 'easier' side. Then work on the opposite one to help him improve flexibility and even up in his movement.

1 Hold some treats in one hand at waist level, with your clicker in the other hand held in a similar position, so that your elbows are at right angles. When your dog realizes that you have treats, he will come towards you. When he reaches a point a couple of steps away from you and is standing fairly straight, click.

2 Instead of giving him the treat, throw it out to your side. Aim for it to land on the floor at least 2 m (6 ft 6 in) away from you. Your dog will go to get the treat.

3 Once he has eaten that treat, he will return to see if you have any more. As he does so he will start to look up to your hands or face.

Key points

● Aim to get your dog returning to you, placing his front paws in front of you and then smartly swinging round on his hindlegs to straighten his body and improve his back-end awareness (see page 26).

● Work in an area where the floor is clear so that your dog can easily find his reward and is unlikely to find anything else tempting. He will then quickly realize that you are the best source of treats.

4 He may stop initially at right angles to you or he may swing round to stand straight in front you. Click when he steps his hindlegs round to bring his body straight so that he is facing you. Then throw his treat to the opposite side to repeat the exercise again. Gradually ask for a straighter body position and a faster return to you by withholding the click.

5 Continue to repeat the exercise so that your dog learns that it is how he returns to you that is important. Then try turning 90 degrees away from your dog each time you have thrown the reward. This will compel him to flex and step around more to position himself in front of you. Once your dog is positioning himself squarely in front of you, add the 'in front' command just before you click and reward.

Move along

THE TRICK
- Dog and owner face each other and sidestep in unison

Once your dog understands the 'in front' position (see page 64), you can develop this into sidestepping together, facing one another. Begin by reinforcing the 'in front' position whichever way you are facing and then begin to introduce sideways movement, too.

As you begin to sidestep, move with a spring in your step and keep a rhythm. If you can, take a step to the side, then cross your other leg in front before taking another sidestep. This will look much more polished. Try taking three steps to the side, then kick to the side before changing direction.

1 First, practise this exercise based on a clock face, as it should help your dog separate out the movement he needs to make with his hindquarters from that of his forequarters. Imagine you are at the centre of the clock face and your dog is one of the hands. Start at two o'clock and then, as you give the command 'in front', swivel round to face four o'clock.

⭐ Working on both sides

Dogs tend to have a favoured side and may even move differently in one direction compared to the other. On the 'easier' side, they will tend to cross their hindlegs over, while on the harder side they may step the foot up to the other one but not cross it. Usually dogs will find sidestepping to the right more difficult, especially if they have not been taught to move into the heel position on both sides (see page 32). Practise all exercises regularly in both directions to ensure even muscle build-up and maximize suppleness.

2 Aim for your dog to take big sideways steps with his hindlegs. Click for the strongest ones and reward. Now move round to six and eight o'clock in the same way, before trying the movements in an anticlockwise direction. Observe which way your dog finds easiest.

3 Now, try taking a sidestep in the direction your dog finds the easiest. Command 'in front' and keep your hands positioned as you did previously for that move (see Step 1, page 64). As your dog steps across with his hindlegs, click and then treat.

4 Repeat the move, aiming to get your dog to step across equally with his front and back legs. Ask for two steps before clicking and treating. As he learns to step through well, gradually increase the number of steps and the speed, and introduce changes of direction.

Key points

● Do this move to some upbeat music, as this will help you keep a good rhythm and add to the fun.

● Make your sideways steps decisive and active to encourage your dog to move positively.

● Try to click when your dog's hindquarters are in line with the centre of your body.

● Make sure you have enough space to move freely without bumping into furniture or walls. In confined areas, your dog may feel intimidated and so become reluctant to move.

Round the twist

The twist move can be done on the spot or built into a sequence on the move. However, to ensure that your dog is able to keep travelling forwards as well as doing a twist, it is important to teach the move with the correct hand for each side of the body. This way, your dog can move forwards into the turn and come out of it facing the right direction to continue onwards. This will also allow you to indicate which direction twist you want by the hand you use.

To make sure you get the correct hand, think of doing the breaststroke – with your right hand, you circle clockwise, and with the left, anticlockwise. The same principle applies to this trick.

1 With your dog standing in front of you, hold a treat to his nose with your right hand. Encourage him to turn his head to the right by moving the treat level with his nose backwards as far as his shoulder. Once he has flexed this far, click and treat.

2 Now lure his head round further towards his tail, until he takes a step with his front feet. As he steps, click and reward.

Key points

● Once your dog can complete a full twist, encourage him to keep twisting by withholding the click to a twist-and-a-quarter, two twists and so on.

● If you get into a knot with the luring, check that you are using the right hand for the direction in which you want your dog to turn.

● Take your lead from your dog as to how fast to twist, then build up speed gradually.

● Don't forget to teach the move in the opposite direction, too. Use the opposite hand to lure and give this move a separate command. For example, say 'twist' for a clockwise turn and 'spin' for an anticlockwise turn.

● Once your dog has mastered the twist in front of you, try it to either side and then have a go at walking and asking him to twist, before walking on again.

3 This time, ask for more of a turn by luring your dog's nose past his tail position so that he has to step round with front and hindlegs. As soon as he passes the halfway mark, click. From here your dog is likely to continue the circle of his own accord so that he comes round to face you and so receive his reward.

4 Once he is facing you and standing straight, reward. Repeat this exercise several times until you can complete a full circle in one flowing move, clicking as he passes the halfway point and rewarding as he faces you. You should be able to stop using a lure quite quickly and just make the hand movement. Once he has got the idea, add the command 'twist' or 'spin' before you click and treat. You can then stand up, give the 'twist' command and without a hand signal your dog will spin on the spot.

Sticking around

This move forms the basis of other circular moves,
such as circling around one leg (see page 75) or
a cane (see page 82), and helps prepare him for
more complicated tricks, such as weaving
through your legs (see page 78).

To teach your dog to circle around you
fluently, you must make sure you are able to
transfer the lure you use quickly and smoothly
between hands. If you hesitate or fumble, your
dog will lose the flow of movement or become
distracted or confused. Try practising passing
your lure, hand to hand, in front and
behind your body, clockwise and
anticlockwise, before you start
working your dog.

⭐ Keeping it positive

Tune the length of your practice
sessions to your dog. If he is happy
and enjoying himself, continue, but
make sure you call an end to the
session while things are still going
well – your dog will then be keen
to come back for more. If things
are going badly, he could be
confused, bored or tired. Change
to a trick your dog knows well,
perform it once and reward him.
You can then finish the session on
a high note and come back to the
harder task when you are both
feeling fresh.

1 Begin with your dog
standing at heel on
your left side (see page 32).
Hold the treat and clicker in
your right hand and lure
your dog across the front of
you, around your right side.

Key points

● If passing the treats from one hand to the other proves tricky, try having some in each hand.

● For this type of move, using a toy can be more effective and easier than food, as long as your dog responds well to it.

● Teach this move in the opposite direction, too, using the opposite hand sequence. Use a different voice command so that you can signal which way you wish your dog to move.

● With a small dog, it may be easier to teach this move from a kneeling position.

● Once your dog is circling well around you, you can vary the trick by simultaneously turning in the opposite direction to him.

2 Bring your dog around behind you and smoothly switch your lure from one hand to the other, keeping your dog moving.

3 As soon as your dog is following your left hand around towards the left side of your body, click.

4 Encourage your dog to complete the circle around you, bringing him back to his starting position beside you, and treat. Repeat this sequence two or three times, each time clicking after you transfer the lure to the other hand, but treating at different points in the circle, not just at heel. Now add in the verbal command 'round' and gradually stop luring with food or a toy, instead just making the same hand movements to direct your dog. Once your dog has learned the voice command, you can then fade out the hand signals if you wish.

The magic circle

When done well, this trick can look as if the dog is on the end of a long piece of invisible string that keeps him connected to his owner. How wide a circle your dog traces will depend on the space you have available and the size of circle you teach him initially.

Having taught your dog to circle close to you (see page 70), you now need to teach him to move much further away. This is best done with a puppy pen (page 11), as this provides a solid but see-through barrier that can be adjusted to different shapes and sizes. For really big circles, you may need to use two puppy pens joined together.

1 Set up your pen in a wide circle and get into the enclosed area. Using a treat, lure your dog around the outside of the pen by walking around the perimeter.

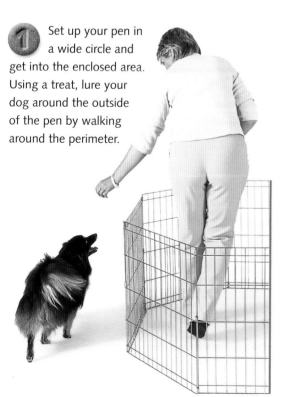

2 Once your dog has begun to move, begin to throw treats a few steps in front of him every few strides. As he starts to move forward well to get the treats, click just before he reaches them. Complete several circuits like this and then add in the verbal command 'go out' or 'wide' before clicking and throwing a treat.

3 When your dog understands the command, try rotating in the centre of the circle. Give the voice command, click as your dog moves, throwing food ahead for him to treat and maintain the movement. Once the movement is flowing, reduce and vary the amount of food you throw. For example, after half a circle, click and treat, then a circle-and-a-half, then one circle, then two circles. This will teach your dog to circle continuously until you say otherwise.

Adding a counter-turn

Develop this trick by turning in a circle yourself, in the opposite direction to your dog. When first introducing this movement, wait until your dog has just gone past your line of sight to the side and turn half a circle. Keep repeating this until you can start to turn full circles without distracting your dog.

4 When your dog can be cued to circle from a verbal command, try the move without the puppy pen. Keep your dog out wide by always clicking at the furthest point he reaches and throwing a treat out to him. If he does keep coming in close, throw a treat out to move him away and then click just before he reaches it.

Key points

● Don't worry if you throw the food wide as long as it is in front of your dog, as he will soon return to circling again.

● If your dog insists on coming close to you once you remove the pen, put the barrier back in place and practise a little more.

● Teach this trick moving in both directions, giving a different command for each.

Through the legs

As well as needing to be flexible and able to move well, to perform some of the more complex tricks, a dog needs to be confident that their owner is careful and isn't about to stand on them. This trick helps both to establish trust and improve suppleness.

1 With your dog in a wait in front of you (see page 30), stand with your legs wide enough apart for your dog to fit through comfortably. Place a treat through your legs and onto the floor 2.5–5 cm (1–2 in) behind you. Call your dog, and as soon as his nose goes through your legs but before he gets the treat, click. If he reverses back after getting his reward, don't worry.

2 Repeat, gradually placing or throwing the food further behind you until your dog goes right through your legs. Click as he passes under you. As he gets his food, turn to face him and throw another treat through your legs so that your dog passes back under you the other way. Repeat this to encourage your dog to move quickly. Once he is confident, add the command 'through' before you click.

Round one leg

THE TRICK

● Dog circles around either of owner's legs on command

This helps to build the confidence that is essential if your dog is to learn to move around your legs as you are moving – for example, weaving through your legs as you walk (see page 78) – as well as improving his flexibility.

Key points

● If your dog keeps going around your legs instead of through the gap between them, reduce the distance you are throwing the food to slow things down.

● Make it easy for your dog by giving him plenty of room and making the route clear by keeping your hair, head, clothing and arms out of the way.

● Aim for your dog to come through your legs straight, quickly and cleanly.

● Try using a button clicker (see page 10), which can be operated more easily within your hand when you are holding treats.

1 To circle the left leg, begin with your dog on your left side. Holding the clicker in your right hand and treats in both hands, lure your dog around the front of you and then between your legs. Switch your dog from the food in your right to that in your left hand, and as soon as he goes through your legs, click.

2 Bring your dog around your left side with your left hand until he is back where he started and treat. Repeat this several times, and once your dog gets the idea, reduce the luring and click and treat at different points of the circle to encourage continuous movement. Add in the command 'through, round' so that your dog knows he is to go through your legs first and then circle. Once your dog links the command to the move, he should be able to do it with you standing upright. Don't forget to then teach him to circle your right leg anticlockwise, using the reverse hand sequence.

Ins and outs

THE TRICK

● Dog circles owner's legs in a figure-of-eight pattern on command

Before trying this move, make sure your dog can circle around each of your legs well (anticlockwise around the right leg and clockwise around the left – see page 75) and is confident going through your legs (see page 74). By teaching these moves first, you will be more likely to avoid problems such as your dog missing out part of the figure-of-eight move or hesitating because he is unsure of the pattern you want.

Once you have cracked this first weave move where you are static, the foundation is laid for the various weave tricks that involve you and your dog being on the move.

1 With your dog on your left, lure him around the front of your left leg using a treat in your left hand. Switch him over to follow the treat in your right hand, positioned behind your right knee, to encourage him through your legs.

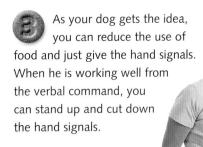 Lure him with your right hand around your right leg. Swap your dog back to following your left hand, positioned behind your left knee, and lead him back through your legs. Click as he passes under this time. Bring him back around your left leg with your left hand to the starting point and treat. Practise so the move flows. Vary where and how soon you click and treat to encourage continuity, and add in the command 'weave'.

As your dog gets the idea, you can reduce the use of food and just give the hand signals. When he is working well from the verbal command, you can stand up and cut down the hand signals.

Keep practising and your dog will get faster and be able to weave around your legs from just the verbal command.

Key points

● To help your dog weave through your legs, flex the knee that you want him to go behind forwards. This makes the gap a little bit clearer and more inviting to him.

● Initially, aim to click as your dog passes under your legs for the second time, to complete the figure-of-eight.

● As you first teach the weave, make sure you don't move the hand holding the treat too fast, as your dog will try to cut corners to get it.

Weave walking

For this trick to look good, concentrate
on your own body position. Avoid
slumping or shuffling; instead walk tall,
proud and with purpose.

Before having a go, make sure your
dog can weave on the spot (see page 76)
from your voice command. This avoids
you having to try to lean down and lure
your dog while standing on one leg.

1 Begin with your dog on your
left. Raise your right leg and
command 'weave'. As your dog
passes under your leg, begin to make
the step forward.

2 As your right foot reaches the
floor, command 'weave' again
to encourage your dog to come back
under your other leg.

3 Raise your left leg and click as
your dog passes underneath.
Give him a treat once he reaches your
left side again. Now build up the
number of steps before clicking and
treating your dog on either side of you.

Sidestep weaving

To begin with, you will need to slow things down to let your dog get an idea of what's required, so practise walking a step at a time, balancing on each leg in turn. Your dog won't appreciate you wobbling about or falling over him.

Key points

● Always hold the leg you wish your dog to pass under out in front of you. It can seem easier to step forwards and leave a leg behind for your dog to weave under, but this looks messy and awkward once you begin to speed up.

● If you get mixed up with your steps, practise these first before trying them with your dog.

1 With your dog on your left, raise your leg in front of you, telling your dog to 'weave'. As he passes under your leg, swing your right leg across your left leg. Step sideways with left leg, cross right leg over the left leg again.

2 Now lift your left leg in front of you, commanding 'weave' so that he passes under this leg in the opposite direction. As he goes under, click. Then cross your left leg in front of your right to again sidestep to the right. As your dog turns to come to you, treat. Gradually build up this sequence and practise in both directions.

Kick it!

THE TRICK

● Owner dances to the side and dog weaves through legs on first and last step

1 With your dog on your right, kick your left leg out in front of you and command him to 'weave'.

This move is great fun and ideal for getting a lazy or slower dog into action. Although you need to be quite quick on your feet, your dog doesn't have to be so fast to weave correctly. There is plenty of movement and excitement to stimulate him and therefore more chance of him achieving the goal.

Read through the steps before you have a go, as they are different to sideways weaving (see page 79) and need a little more coordination. Think about moving in a good rhythm by saying to yourself '1-2-3 kick', then put on some upbeat music and strut your stuff!

2 As your dog goes under your left leg, bring it across your right leg to sidestep to your right.

3 Take another step to your right with your right leg.

Key points

● Take care not to tread on your dog's feet.

● Start slowly and build up the speed once your dog understands what you want.

● To begin with, click and treat once your dog has completed the second weave. Then increase the exercise so that you move in both directions before clicking and so on.

● If your dog gets too excited, work through a couple of calmer exercises before doing this one again.

4 Cross-step with your left leg again…

5 …and finish with a right-leg kick to the front, commanding your dog to 'weave'. Then simply cross-step with your right leg to the left to repeat the sequence in the opposite direction. Phew!

Pole position

By introducing your dog to working with a pole, you can begin to add in all sorts of extras to your tricks. You can get your dog to jump it, go under it, go round it or even use it to give directions or create new movements.

To begin with, the pole will be used to introduce tricks that you can later perform with a cane. At this stage, it is vital to use a free-standing pole to avoid confusing your dog and allow you two free hands. You can either buy poles with cone bases from agility suppliers or make your own version (see page 11).

1 With the pole and your dog on your right, lure your dog away from you and around the far side of the pole with your right hand.

2 Encourage him all the way round and click just before he completes the circle, then reward. Repeat this several times, building up to two or three circles before clicking and rewarding. Add the command 'circle pole' or 'pole' before clicking.

⭐ Performance planning

Always think about how you plan to use a trick before you teach it. If you are hoping to use it in a sequence, the direction in which you teach your dog can be critical. By teaching the circles in the directions described here, you'll be able to walk, plant your cane and circle in the opposite direction to your dog. If they are taught the opposite ways, you will not be able to flow into this move, instead having to turn around and change hands on your cane to get the same effect.

3 Now cut down your hand movements until your dog will still circle with your hand just resting on the top of the pole.

4 Once your dog understands the move and the verbal command in one direction, teach the other side. On your left, your dog should circle the pole clockwise.

5 Once your dog is confident with the move, you can try moving in a circle in the opposite direction to him. When this is fluent, you can have a go with a proper cane.

Key points

● Teach this trick with a free-standing pole. It isn't possible to lure your dog and hold the pole upright without getting in a big tangle and confusing your dog.

● Teach the circle moves around you first (see pages 70–73) so that your dog already understands the basic idea.

● Toys can be better lures for this trick, as they are more visible.

Swing it!

Teach this move using two free-standing poles initially, so your dog learns the figure-of-eight pattern. He should already be able to circle one pole and understand that the direction he circles depends on which side of your body you hold the pole (see page 82). By linking these skills together one flowing move will be created. For a slick trick, progress to using a single cane and just think Fred Astaire!

 Stand between and slightly behind the two poles, spaced so that you can reach past both of them. With your dog on your left and the lure in your left hand, lead him clockwise round the left pole, commanding 'pole' or 'circle pole'.

2 As he turns back towards you, switch your dog onto the lure in your right hand. Lead him anticlockwise round the right pole and again command 'pole'.

3 Take him around the right pole, and as he comes round to face you, lead your dog across to the other pole by swapping him back onto the lure in your left hand. Take him around the left pole, and as he reaches his starting point, click and reward. Repeat this sequence, building up how much your dog has to do to get a click. With practice, you will be able to reduce the luring and hand movement until you can simply place your hand on the top of the pole that you wish your dog to circle.

4 Once your dog knows to circle the pole that your hand is on, try using a cane. First hold it out to your right and command 'pole' so that your dog circles it…

5 …then switch the cane to the other hand across your body…

6 …before placing the pole to your left and commanding your dog so that he circles in the opposite direction.

Key points

● In time, you will be able to drop the verbal command completely, as the positioning of the cane will cue your dog.

● If your dog is new to circling moves or is unsure of what you are asking for, break the move down into small steps. Send your dog around the left pole and click as he returns to you and reward. Then send him around the right pole, clicking as he comes back towards you and treating. You can then link the two circles together.

● Once your dog has learned the trick, you can try different props, such as an umbrella.

Backtrack

Tricks and sequences involving backward moves look dramatic, and many dogs will learn to reverse quite quickly. As well as being good for performing, a dog who can reverse easily will be less cumbersome in the house, as he will be able to manoeuvre out of your path more readily. Reversing can be taught in several different ways.

Method 1
In this approach, food is used to prompt the behaviour, while the dog is allowed to work out what is required by himself.

1 With your feet wide enough apart for your dog to fit between them, place a treat between your heels. Let your dog come and get it. Once he has eaten it, he is likely to step backwards so that he can look up to your hands or face to see if more food is coming.

2 As soon as he takes a step back, click and reward him with another treat placed between your feet. Repeat until your dog gets the idea. Once your dog is reversing back to look at you, try withholding the click. He is likely to reverse to the same point, wait for the click, but when none comes, try another step or two backwards. Click as soon as he does this and reward again between your feet. Continue to increase the number of steps in this way. Once your dog is walking backwards well, add the command 'walk back', then gradually cut out the treat being placed on the floor.

Method 2

In this method, you use your body position and hand movement to 'push' your dog into walking backwards.

1 With your dog standing in front of you, hold a treat to his nose. Keeping your hand level, make a quick, firm but gentle pushing movement with the food into your dog's muzzle. You are aiming to encourage him to tuck his head backwards into his neck.

⭐ Keeping on the straight and narrow

To help keep your dog straight as he reverses, use the 'in front' command (see page 64), as your dog should have learned to move his hindlegs in line with his front legs as part of this move. Alternatively, make a channel using a puppy pen (see pages 11 and 88). Get him confident moving forwards through the channel first, then as he reverses he will have a low fence on either side to guide him back.

2 At the same time, step towards your dog – your body and hand movement should encourage him to move backwards. As soon as he takes a step, click and treat. Practise, gradually increasing the number of steps, and then add in the 'walk back' command.

 ### Key points

● **Keeping a good hand position is critical – too high and your dog will sit; too low and he will simply lie down.**

● **Your hand needs to move at the right speed – too slow and your dog will just sit or not move at all.**

Reversing in tandem

THE TRICK

- Dog and owner walk backwards, the dog staying in the heel position

As well as reversing away from you, you can teach your dog to reverse with you. This trick is best taught using a puppy pen (see page 11), set up to form a channel, giving your dog a clear guideline of how and where you want him to move, and allowing him to work out the rest by himself. He is then likely to be rewarded more easily and so learn the task more efficiently.

Key points

- Step back confidently yourself.
- Repeat your command regularly to help straighten your dog, once you have moved out of the puppy pen channel.
- If your dog starts to tuck behind you or swings out, practise again with the pen.

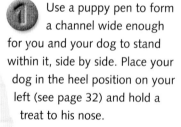

1 Use a puppy pen to form a channel wide enough for you and your dog to stand within it, side by side. Place your dog in the heel position on your left (see page 32) and hold a treat to his nose.

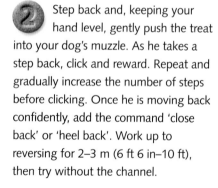

2 Step back and, keeping your hand level, gently push the treat into your dog's muzzle. As he takes a step back, click and reward. Repeat and gradually increase the number of steps before clicking. Once he is moving back confidently, add the command 'close back' or 'heel back'. Work up to reversing for 2–3 m (6 ft 6 in–10 ft), then try without the channel.

Reversing in the round

Key points

● Adjust the size of the pen to suit the size of your dog.

● Make sure you allow enough room in the pen behind you for your dog to reverse.

● If you do not have a pen, use a corner of your kitchen or any other room. You can then teach half a circle of reversing at a time, with your dog moving between you and the corner.

A puppy pen is again used here to guide the required movement, this time to form a circle. Once the basics are in place, you can move on to trying the trick in the open.

1 Create a pen which gives your dog just enough room to move around when you stand in the middle. Walk your dog forwards around you to get him used to the restricted space. Then, starting from the left heel position, command 'back' but remain still. If necessary, encourage your dog to step backwards by gently moving a treat into his nose.

2 As his nose emerges past your right leg, click and give him a treat on your right side. Repeat for the second half of the circle. Build up to your dog completing a full circle before clicking and then withhold the click to achieve several circles in succession. Add a verbal command – either a specific one, such as 'reverse', or a context-related one, such as 'back up, around'.

3 Once your dog can do multiple circles around you in the pen, try without it. If he achieves this, then move on to teaching him the move in the opposite direction, using the same method shown in Steps 1 and 2.

Back up

This trick is really several moves that have all been taught separately and are then linked together to achieve the full effect. To be able to perform the complete sequence, your dog needs to be able to reverse away from you on command, make a half turn and reverse between your legs.

Teach each of these things thoroughly and don't try to do the whole lot at once, or your dog will feel bombarded. A more gradual approach will achieve a much better, lasting result.

⭐ Sound support

As your dog backs up, he will struggle to see where you are unless he turns his head, although some dogs do try hard to use their peripheral vision. Therefore, help him locate you with sound by repeating the 'back up' command – some dogs will rely heavily on sound for this move.

1 First teach your dog to reverse through your legs. Stand astride him and, with a treat to his nose, 'push' him gently backwards. Click as he goes through your legs and treat him when he returns to your side. Repeat this until he does it without the 'push', then add the command 'back up'.

2 Gradually increase the distance you ask your dog to reverse to reach you. Begin just a stride away – give the command and click as your dog goes through your legs, rewarding once he is at your side again. Then build up by telling your dog to 'stand, wait' and walking back behind him, adding a stride at a time until he can reverse to you across a room.

Key points

● Your dog is likely to reverse into you to begin with, so try to move to accommodate him.

● Keep your turn tidy to increase the chances of your dog reversing accurately to you.

● As you link the components of the trick together, watch for signs that your dog doesn't understand. It is better to slow down a little or return to the previous step and get minor problems ironed out before they become major ones.

3 Now teach the half turn. Begin with your dog facing you and lure him around as if doing a twist (see page 68).

4 Once your dog is facing away from you, click and throw a treat in front of him so he doesn't have to do a full circle to get the reward. If he continues past 180 degrees, put your hand on his hindquarters to stop him. Practise and add in the command 'turn'. Once your dog turns on command, link it to the back up. With your dog in a 'stand, wait', move a few steps ahead of him. Tell him to 'turn' and then 'back up', clicking as he passes through your legs. Establish this then add the commands 'walk back', 'turn' and finally 'back up'.

Jump to it!

Teaching your dog to jump gives you another whole dimension of fun. By starting low, your dog learns how to take off and land correctly, without risking injury. You can then gradually increase the height of the obstacles and he will be able to tackle them safely. Don't be tempted to push your dog too much – a jump of 0.7 m (2 ft 6 in) is plenty even for a large, fit dog with agility experience.

Don't forget, too, to take your dog's age, fitness and health into consideration. If you have any doubts, ask your vet to check him over to give him clearance for take-off!

⭐ Staying focused

For a dog to jump well, his front paws should take off first and land first. He can only do this if he is looking in the direction he is travelling. You often see dogs bounce over fences, landing either with all four feet together or hindlegs first. This is because they are looking up to their owner, rather than concentrating on the job in hand. As a result, the dog may hit fences or land poorly, increasing his risk of injury. It will also lose time in agility competitions.

1 Set up a jump 5–15 cm (2–6 in) high so that it is easy for your dog to get over and impossible for him to get under. Command your dog to wait (see page 30) while you step over the jump and take a couple of strides before turning to face your dog. Recall him enthusiastically with your arms held wide, clicking as he takes the jump and treating once he reaches you. Repeat several times, adding in the command 'over'.

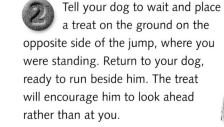

② Tell your dog to wait and place a treat on the ground on the opposite side of the jump, where you were standing. Return to your dog, ready to run beside him. The treat will encourage him to look ahead rather than at you.

③ Release and run with him as he goes over the jump to get the treat. Click as he jumps. Practise this and then try sending him over the jump without running beside him. He should still go over the jump to get the treat. Gradually, you can stop placing treats on the floor and ask for several jumps before rewarding your dog.

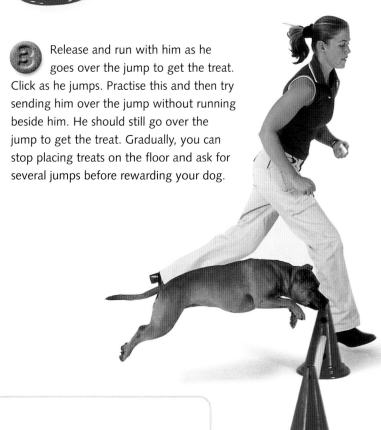

⭐ Fancy footwork

Once your dog understands the 'over' command, sit on the floor with your legs outstretched and your dog beside you. Throw a treat to the opposite side and command 'over'. He will soon learn to hop over your legs – click as he does so and repeat in the opposite direction. This can be developed to a standing position, with your dog jumping the crook of your foot.

Spread your wings

Once your dog jumps basic obstacles, you can teach him to leap all sorts of things. To teach him to jump over your arm, you need a helper, to show your dog what is wanted and help him to jump accurately. He needs to leap over your arm, not just your hand, and to look forwards rather than at you. Get together with a dog-owning friend so you can both benefit, and even try getting both dogs to jump at once.

1 Ask your helper to kneel and hold their arm out straight and low. With your dog in a wait (see page 30), hold a treat close to his nose. Release him and run, aiming to stay a step ahead, using your body position to guide him over the outstretched arm. Click as he jumps and reward when he catches up. Repeat several times.

2 If your dog is confident, ask your helper to gradually raise their arm height until it is at shoulder level. Practise jumping in both directions and on both sides of your helper's body.

3 Position your dog in a wait in front of your helper, and go behind them so that you are taking your dog across the outstretched arm. Call your dog towards you and command 'over', clicking as he jumps the arm and rewarding as he reaches you. Practise this so that your dog jumps accurately.

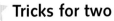

★ Tricks for two

Once your dog is confident jumping, you can teach him all sorts of variations to make your tricks more effective. If you have two dogs, try asking one dog to 'down, wait' while the other circles you, jumping the first dog. Make sure the dogs are of suitable sizes and temperaments first!

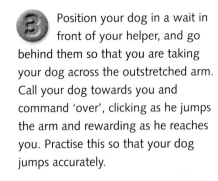

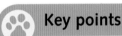

🐾 Key points

● Keep a stride ahead of your dog when running with him, to give him room to see the jump and judge the distance. If your hand is less than 15 cm (6 in) from his nose, he will only focus on the treat.

● If your dog dives around your helper's outstretched arm, reposition yourself so that your dog is channelled over the jump.

● You can build up the trick so that your dog jumps one arm in one direction and your other arm back again. Use a helper to show him how to make the turn.

● Your dog may jump your arm in either direction, but start with him coming towards you for ease.

4 Now you or your helper can try the trick alone. With your dog in a wait, kneel several strides in front of him and raise your arm. Command your dog 'over', clicking as he jumps your arm and throwing rewards ahead of him.

Ring master

Teach your dog to jump through a hoop as a trick in itself or as the starting point to jumping through your arms. Once he knows what the hoop is for, you can build up sequences where he moves around you, jumping through the hoop each time you present it.

1 Introduce your dog to the hoop by asking him to walk through it at floor level. Click once his front half is through and treat once his whole body is clear. Raise the hoop 5–7.5 cm (2–3 in) off the floor and again encourage your dog through. Click once the front half of his body has emerged and treat when he is fully through. Gradually build up the height and introduce the command 'through' or 'hoop' before the click.

2 Encourage your dog to jump higher and faster by asking him to wait and throwing a treat on the floor on the opposite side of the hoop. Release him and command 'hoop', clicking as he jumps through. With practice, you will be able to drop the verbal command, as simply holding out the hoop will cue your dog.

Jumping duo

THE TRICK

● Dog jumps through owner's arm held in a hoop shape

When your dog is confident with jumping through a hoop, try this harder jump through your arms. You'll need someone to help you teach this trick, but the end result is a great illustration of you and your dog's teamwork and trust in one another.

Key points

● Avoid wearing baggy clothes or having floppy hair when asking your dog to jump through your arms – he needs to be able to see a clear space to jump through.

● Whether holding out a hoop or your arms, keep a steady position so that your dog can judge where he is expected to jump.

● The higher you are asking your dog to jump, the bigger run-up you need to give him.

1 Ask your dog to 'sit, wait' and position yourself a few paces in front of him. Make a big hoop with your arms, low to the ground, and ask your helper to stand on the landing side and show your dog a treat through the centre of the circle, with the hand nearest to your dog. Command 'hoop', and as soon as your dog takes off to go through your arms, click. Your helper then throws the food to land a few paces ahead of your dog. Repeat.

2 Using the same method, slowly build up the height. Once you have clicked, your helper should continue to throw the treat ahead of your dog to keep him focused and travelling forwards.

3 If your dog is confident going through your arms towards your helper and understands the verbal command, try the trick without your friend's extra encouragement. Start with a treat placed on the floor on the landing side, or your helper standing near you ready to throw a treat. Make a hoop with your arms and command him to jump. As he jumps, click. With practice, your arm position will become the cue for your dog to jump.

Get a wiggle on

> **THE TRICK**
> ● Dog weaves in and out of a straight row
>   of upright poles

If you want your dog to be a flexible friend, there is no better exercise than this. The weave poles are a highlight of every agility ring, with the best dogs appearing to be just a blur as they complete this task. To get to this level takes lots of practice, but even doing this exercise steadily will improve your dog's coordination and ability to bend.

1 Begin with your dog at your right side at one end of the poles. You will walk along the left side of the poles while your dog goes in and out of them. Lure him away from you and anticlockwise around the first pole, bringing him between the first and second pole. Then go clockwise around the second pole, between the second and third pole, and so on along the line.

2 As his nose goes between the last pair of poles, click, rewarding as he clears them completely. Repeat this several times.

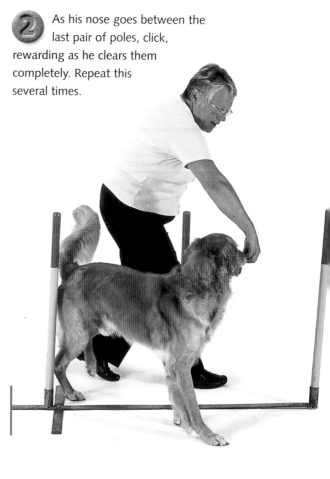

3 As your dog gets the idea, he should be happy to just follow your hand for guidance. Add the command 'weave' for each turn about a pole.

⭐ Fast-tracking

For agility competitions, dogs are always expected to enter the weave poles with the first pole by their left shoulder. To focus them on travelling quickly, straight through the poles, the exercise is often taught using a channel. The weave poles are set up in two lines just wide enough for the dog to fit through the middle, within the channel. Once the dog has learned to travel down the centre of them, they are moved slightly closer so that he has to wiggle his body slightly. This is increased until he has to slalom fully, but he is focused on getting through the poles rather than on moving from side to side.

4 Click as he goes between the last two poles, and throw the treat ahead of your dog to encourage him to come through the poles faster. Practise this, building up speed and reducing your hand signals, until you can just move your hand in a straight line and give the command. Eventually even the visual cue can be dropped.

Follow your leader

To train your dog successfully, you need to tap into how he would naturally solve problems. Your dog has three main tools he can use – his nose, his mouth or his paws. Clicker training encourages dogs to use all of these to work out the answer to the tasks we set.

We can train a dog specifically to use his foot, nose or mouth on cue. This is done by using 'targets' that the dog is trained to touch with a specific part of his body. The target can then be moved and used in various situations to transfer the behaviour to other items or to teach complex moves. In effect, the target tells your dog to put that bit of his body, such as his nose, here.

Start by teaching your dog to place his nose on or close to your hand. This will give you an easy way to guide him through moves such as heelwork without the use of luring.

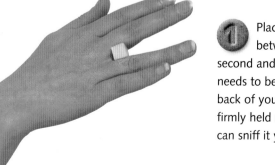

1 Place a piece of food between your second and third fingers. It needs to be visible from the back of your hand, but firmly held so that your dog can sniff it yet not get it.

Choosing your target

Think of targeting as another tool in your training repertoire – you don't have to use it, but you may find that it makes certain tricks easier to teach. There are three main types of target used in dog training:

1 Your hand A good starting point, suitable for close work such as heeling and twists. It takes away the need to hold a toy or treat, so looks neater and smoother.

2 Target stick This extendable stick (see pages 11 and 102) is particularly suited to teaching wider circle moves and standing on hindlegs, and can be used to elevate your dog's movement to create a high-stepping trot. It is great for working with small dogs, as it saves bending.

3 Target marker Usually a flat object such as a mat, plastic lid or piece of wood, which you can teach your dog to touch with a paw or nose (see pages 11 and 103). The marker can be moved onto another object to show your dog how and where you want him to touch it. Ideal for prop-based moves such as skateboarding (see page 118) or pushing a ball (see page 108).

2 Hold the back of your hand out to your dog so that he sniffs at the treat. As soon as he touches his nose on your hand, click and move your target hand upwards out of his reach. Give a treat from your other hand before presenting your target hand again slightly in front of him so that he comes to sniff it again. Click and treat as before.

3 Gradually ask your dog to move further to touch your hand and throw his treats a little way from you to encourage faster movement. Then try presenting your hand without a treat between your fingers. If your dog still touches your hand, click and treat. Repeat and add a verbal command such as 'pat' or 'nose' and build up how far your dog moves before clicking. Once he has the idea, you should be able to move your hand in any direction and your dog will follow.

Key points

● If your dog doesn't touch the target within three seconds of you presenting it, move it out of reach again. Then re-present your target hand, showing the food in it, and encouraging your dog by asking 'what's this?'.

● Once your dog follows a target, make sure you continue to click and treat at intervals to maintain his motivation.

Targeted moves

Teaching your dog to move to a target is all about telling him exactly what, where and how you want him to interact with an object. The target stick and marker are both used for this, but each works better for different situations. The target stick is good for creating movement in a specific direction.

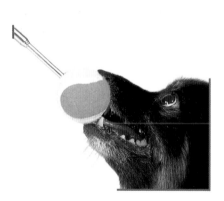

Nose target

Stick a small ball on the end of the target stick to make it more visible and easier to touch. With the clicker and target stick in the same hand, hold the stick out near your dog. As soon as his nose touches it to sniff, click. Throw a treat in the opposite direction so that he then has to move back to the stick to touch it again. Practise then add the command 'pat' before clicking.

Stand and bow

Once your dog has learned to follow the target stick fluently, it opens up many other ways of encouraging moves. Simply lift the stick up for a stand on back legs or move it down between the dog's legs for a bow. It will also allow you to achieve more accurate circle moves or teach a high-stepping trot.

Paw moves

Cue paw moves by using a different end on your target stick – ideally a flat, rectangular-shaped piece of plastic or wood to support your dog's paw. Simply hold it out to your dog and give your 'give paw' command (see page 36). Click as he touches and then treat. Repeat.

Hitting the mark

- Dog touches marker with his nose or paw

The target marker is used to tell your dog to 'go to' a specific place or touch an item at a particular point or in a particular way. As with the target stick, the target marker can be taught as paw- or nose-specific.

Key points

- If your dog bites the target stick, hold it still until he gets bored and lets go. Then click and reward.

- Nose and paw targets must be kept separate to avoid confusion.

1 Choose a small mat or plastic lid to be a nose marker. Place it on the floor, and with your dog in a wait (see page 30), place a treat on top of the marker.

2 Encourage your dog to get the treat and click as soon as his nose touches the marker. Practise this and add in the command 'nose'. Then try with no treat on the mat. If your dog touches it, click and throw a treat away from the mat, then repeat. If he doesn't touch it, place a treat on the mat a few more times.

3 For a foot marker, use a larger mat. With your dog in a wait, place a treat on the side of the mat furthest away from your dog and encourage him to get it. As he steps onto the mat with both front feet to reach the food, click. Practise and add the command 'on your mark'. Then try without a treat on the mat. If he stands on the mat with two feet, click and reward. If not, practise a bit more.

Fetch and carry

Playing and interacting with your dog is a fun and vital part of dog ownership, but it is much harder if your dog regularly clears off with his toys and refuses to bring them back. Teaching him to retrieve will solve this and add to your trick repertoire.

Some dogs are natural retrievers, while others dislike holding things in their mouths. Gun dogs have this behaviour 'in their blood', while toy breeds are frequently 'mealy-mouthed'. Take this into account as well as your dog's preferences for what he holds in his mouth. While some will carry anything, others will only pick up soft or rubber toys.

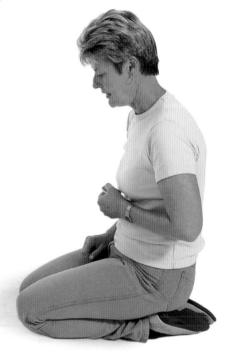

It is easiest to teach retrieving if your dog already understands nose targeting (see page 102).

1 Show your dog the retrieve item, click as he sniffs it and treat. Repeat. Now hold out the toy again, but don't click this time until he mouths it, then treat.

2 Gradually wait a little longer each time before clicking to encourage your dog to keep hold of the toy. Once he holds it for a couple of seconds, try letting go of it yourself. Click before your dog drops the toy and treat. If he drops the toy, wait to see if he picks it up. If he does, click and treat.

3 Put the toy on the floor. If your dog picks it up, click and treat. If not, practise Step 2 a little more. Once your dog is confidently picking up the toy and holding it, try placing it a little further away.

Key points

● Choose a retrieve item that is the right size, weight and material to suit your dog.

● If your dog is carrying the item, withhold the click to increase the distance he brings it – try to click before he drops it.

● If your dog drops the item before you have clicked him for carrying it, wait. He is likely to pick the item up again. You can then click and reward.

● Don't add the 'fetch' command until your dog understands the full task, otherwise it could come to mean chewing, mouthing or dropping the retrieve item.

4 Wait until your dog makes a step towards you holding the toy before clicking. Your dog is likely to drop the toy to come and get his treat. Now wait to see if your dog goes back to the toy. If he picks it up, let him take another step towards you before clicking and repeating the process again.

Leave lessons

It is not uncommon for a dog to be taught to leave and retrieve all at the same time – unsurprisingly, this often leads to confusion, with the dog unsure whether to hold or drop his toy. Treat these as two separate tasks. Teach the leave using a tug toy so that you always remain in control. Play vigorously and then stop and command 'leave'. Simply keep the toy still and boring until your dog lets go, then click and treat. This can be taught from puppyhood.

5 Gradually build up how far your dog brings the toy, until he returns to you in one go. Once he can do this, add the command 'fetch'. Finally, teach your dog to keep hold of the toy until you take it. Once your dog brings the item to you, he may drop it when you click. Simply wait and don't treat. He is then likely to pick up the item – take it from him quietly and reward.

Free time

THE LESSON

● Owner encourages dog to think for himself and offer various behaviours to achieve a reward

The real beauty of clicker training is the flexible and two-way learning it encourages. Its full power to engage your dog is best seen when you give your dog free time. Here, you allow your dog to think for himself, try different behaviours and work out how he can get rewards. It will build confidence and curiosity, as well as improve his comprehension and ability to learn. It will also teach you a lot about your dog – what moves he favours, whether he likes to use a paw or his mouth and just how smart he is.

Free time will show you all sorts of moves that your dog can do which can then be rewarded and cued. For variety, sessions can be done with and without props.

1 Place your prop, like the basket here, on the floor. Then sit down with a pot of treats to indicate to your dog that it's free time. He will soon learn that's his cue to do whatever he wants to earn rewards. Throw a treat into the basket to indicate this is what you are interested in. Now just stay quiet and wait. Here, Gypsy jumps into the basket, so is clicked before she gets the treat.

2 We wait again to see what she does next. She stands up on the edge of the basket, so is clicked for that new behaviour and thrown a treat on the floor.

3 Next she tries standing up with a paw on the handle of the basket. Again, she is clicked for a new behaviour and thrown a treat.

4 Now she jumps in again and lies down, so is clicked and given a treat again. Continue to reward your dog for being creative by recognizing different behaviours.

5 You can then 'zoom in' on a behaviour you like by only rewarding that one, such as paws up on basket handle. This can be refined to two paws on the basket handle by clicking only for both paws. You can then add a command so that you can cue that particular behaviour again.

Key points

● With free time, maintain the momentum by keeping your dog moving – throw the treats in different directions.

● Don't 'zoom in' on a behaviour too quickly or your dog will become stuck and stop offering new moves.

● Reward anything to build your dog's confidence and creativity.

● Remain quiet and still – it's your dog's time in control.

● Dogs early in training or new to free time will offer less than experienced dogs, as they do not yet have a repertoire of possible behaviours to draw on.

● Observe your dog.

Capturing the moment

The clicker can be used to 'capture' naturally occurring behaviours. Simply by observing your dog so that you understand when he is about to do something, you can have your clicker ready and mark behaviours such as yawns, stretching and scratching. Practise and add a cue to enable you to recall the 'natural' behaviour when you want it.

Have a ball

THE TRICK

● Dog 'dribbles' football with his nose and scores a 'goal' between owner's legs.

Most dog's love balls, so tricks involving one are usually greeted enthusiastically. Teaching your dog to play soccer is fun for both of you, and family and friends can join in, too.

For tricks, choose your ball carefully. It needs to be light enough not to hurt your dog if it hits him and so that it readily moves, but strong enough to take his weight and any particularly boisterous play. Make sure it is big enough not to be easily picked up in his mouth and held.

If your dog already understands about using his nose to touch things (see page 102), he will find this trick easier. By teaching it as a nose trick, he will be less likely to mouth or bite the ball.

1 With your dog watching and in a wait, put a treat on the floor and place the ball on top of it.

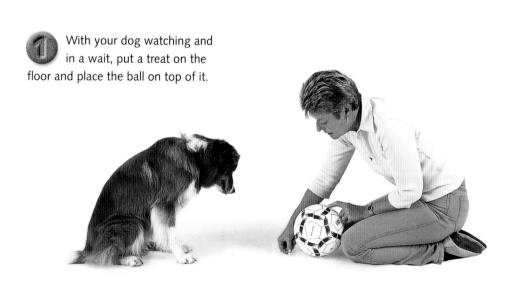

2 Release your dog to get the treat, and as soon as his nose pushes the ball, click. Let him find his reward.

Key points

● If your dog doesn't nudge the ball straightaway when you stop placing a treat under it, simply wait. Be patient and don't worry about not 'telling' your dog what you want – a minute or two of thinking time is all that he needs.

● If your dog keeps biting at the ball, show him that using his nose is more rewarding. Click and reward only when he pushes it with his nose and withhold the click if he uses his teeth.

3 Repeat the sequence, placing treats under the ball in quick succession to build up momentum. This will encourage your dog to stand up and start to move towards the ball.

Goal scoring

Once your dog understands how to push the ball on command, why not add in a 'goal'? Stand close to your dog with your legs apart and command him to push the ball. Click and treat if he manages to put the ball through your legs. Practise this until he understands what you are asking for. You can then add a command 'shoot' and gradually build up the distance he needs to dribble the ball.

4 Once your dog gets the idea, leave out the treat under the ball. Click as soon as your dog pushes the ball and throw a reward to him to keep encouraging movement. When he is readily pushing the ball, add in the command 'push'. Get him to dribble the ball further by withholding the click until he has done two or three nudges – slowly build this up.

Heading the ball

Once your dog can push a ball (see page 108), he will quickly learn how to 'head' it for some really impressive two-way soccer fun.

Don't expect your dog to 'head' the ball as we would – it is still a nose push, but as the ball is now thrown, many dogs will strike the ball with their open jaw.

For this trick to look slick, you will need to be able to throw the ball so that it is just above your dog's head to enable him to 'head' it. The better your throw, the more accurately he will return it and the better your chance of catching it.

1 Hold the ball out to your dog and give the command 'push' (see page 108). When he nudges the ball with his nose, click and treat. Repeat this several times so that your dog is confident about pushing the ball.

2 Command your dog to 'sit, wait' (see page 30) and take a step away from him. With him watching, keep the clicker in one hand and throw the ball so that it goes just above his head. As you throw it, command 'push'.

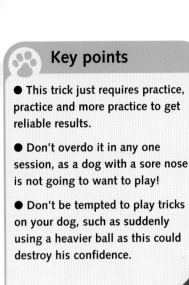

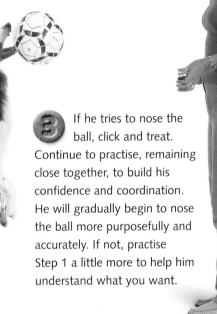

3 If he tries to nose the ball, click and treat. Continue to practise, remaining close together, to build his confidence and coordination. He will gradually begin to nose the ball more purposefully and accurately. If not, practise Step 1 a little more to help him understand what you want.

4 Slowly extend the distance and the height that you throw the ball. As you practise, your dog's 'headers' will become less erratic and more likely to be returned so that you can catch them. Refine his strikes by clicking him only for the ones that come back within your range.

The thrill of the chase

Dogs love balls, as they stimulate their prey drive. In the wild, dogs would hunt for food, and one of the easiest ways for them to identify a potential meal is by looking for movement. Something that moves is likely to be alive and therefore tasty. Balls bring out the hunting instinct as they move with what appears to be a life of their own, so triggering the desire to chase. Other toys just drop to the floor, causing the dog to lose interest.

On the ball

Before trying this trick, make sure your dog understands how to give both his front paws on command (see page 36). Also ensure that the ball is large and strong enough to suit your dog. If it is inflatable, check that it is firm so that it will not give when stood on and will roll easily.

Choose a flat, level surface to teach this trick to enable the ball to move easily when your dog wishes it to, but not before.

 Kneel down in front of your dog and place the ball between you. Hold it steady and give your 'give paw' command (see page 36). As soon as he places a foot on the ball, click and treat. Repeat and then practise with the other paw in the same way.

★ Fancy footwork

All puppies will tend to be very foot-aware and will naturally use their paws to explore any new objects. This is a safety mechanism to literally keep new things at 'arm's length' until they are perceived not to pose a threat. Watch a puppy when it finds a beetle – he will poke it carefully with a paw, ready to leap out of the way if it moves or stings. This way, his sensitive nose will be protected. Many older dogs lose this ability to use their paws, partly perhaps through growing out of it, but also because they are punished for placing a paw on the furniture or standing up on their owner.

Still holding the ball steady, ask your dog for both front feet to be placed on the ball. Give your command for the left paw, and then when this is on the ball, give the 'give paw' command for the right foot. Wait and let your dog work it out. When he does place both paws on the ball, click and treat. If he is still unsure, practise Step 1 a little more. Once your dog is happy placing both paws on the ball, add the command 'on the ball' before you click and treat.

When your dog will work from the verbal command, try standing up. Continue to steady the ball with your foot.

Key points

● Hold the ball still for your dog to start with to encourage his confidence. Don't be tempted to let it roll until your dog really has got the idea.

● Your dog is unlikely to be able to control the ball much to start with, so make sure there is nothing around that he could bump into.

Now try letting the ball roll. Take your foot off, and as soon as the ball moves a tiny way and your dog moves with it, click and treat. Repeat this several times. Gradually let the ball roll a little further before clicking and treating. Build this up until your dog can roll the ball himself.

Stepping up

This trick is an extension of the clock exercise used to teach your dog how to remain 'in front', whichever way you move (see page 64).

Depending on what you have available for your dog to stand up on, you can develop this trick to become all four feet on the podium. Ideally, use something round so that your dog can easily circle it without having to stretch over corners. It also needs to be sturdy, steady and non-slip – a footstool is ideal.

① Place a treat on the stool to indicate to your dog that this is what you are interested in. When his nose touches the stool, click and let him have the treat.

② Now withhold the treat. Wait up to a minute to give your dog the opportunity to work out what else he can do to get a treat. One of the most common responses is to put a paw on the item. If he doesn't, encourage your dog by giving the 'give paw' command (see page 36). As soon as a paw touches the stool, click and throw a treat. Repeat.

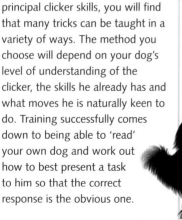

3 Now ask for both front paws on the stool. Either withhold the click once he has one paw up and wait for him to try offering you two paws, or when he has one foot in position, give your other 'give paw' command so that he brings the opposite foot up. When both paws are on the stool, click and throw a treat. Repeat. Once he has got the idea, add in the command 'on the stool' before you click.

Key points

● Make sure your dog has already learned the 'in front' command on the floor (see page 64) before trying it on a stool.

● Practise rotating in both directions around the stool.

● This trick can be taught as 'free time' (see page 106) by using the stool as a prop. Simply click when your dog offers you paws on the stool and when he takes any steps.

● To develop this to four feet on the stool, withhold the click until your dog tries jumping up.

4 Now add the rotation by standing opposite your dog. Face him and take a step around the stool anticlockwise, commanding 'in front'. As your dog moves his hindlegs to swing his hindquarters and remain facing you, click and treat.

5 Take another step and repeat. You can then build up the number of steps taken at a time by withholding the click, until your dog can perform one or more full circles.

Time for bed

This trick has many practical uses as well as entertaining ones. In a hectic household, it is very handy to be able to send your dog to his bed, where you know he will be comfortable and safe. A dog that will settle down without fuss and remain there happily can be a great help. But to achieve this, it is important that your dog is taught to go to his bed in a positive situation, not from anger. This way, he will learn that going to his bed is a good thing, associate it with reward and so not be looking for ways to leave it.

Teaching your dog to 'go to bed' is most easily done as an extended foot target exercise (see page 103). Use a blanket for his bed as the target marker.

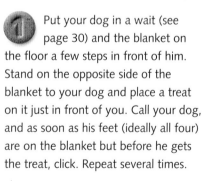

⭐ Transferrable skills

With this task, the blanket becomes, in effect, a foot target and your dog learns that touching it results in rewards. Once he has made the connection to that item, it can be moved to different places and situations, but the task associated with it will remain the same – lie down and settle.

① Put your dog in a wait (see page 30) and the blanket on the floor a few steps in front of him. Stand on the opposite side of the blanket to your dog and place a treat on it just in front of you. Call your dog, and as soon as his feet (ideally all four) are on the blanket but before he gets the treat, click. Repeat several times.

🐾 Key points

● Ask your dog to go a short way to his bed initially, until he understands the task. Once he has the idea, his bed may be in a different room or situation, and he will know to find it.

● Don't expect your dog to necessarily understand if you use a different blanket – a young or inexperienced dog will learn things in close connection to the context. An older dog may work it out easily. If in doubt, refresh your dog's memory of the task with the new bedding.

2 Now repeat Step 1, but after your dog eats the treat, command him 'down' (see page 28). As soon as he lies on the blanket, click and treat again.

3 With your dog in a wait (see page 30), place a treat on the furthest side of the blanket from your dog, but this time return to stand beside him. Now release him and encourage him to get the treat. Click once his feet are on the blanket, but before he reaches the treat. Repeat. Once he is going to the blanket fluently, add the command 'on your bed'.

4 Now repeat Step 3 to send your dog to the blanket, telling him 'on your bed'. Then command your dog 'down' when he is on the blanket. Once he is lying down, click and treat. When your dog has got the idea, stop placing the treat on the blanket.

5 You can now place the blanket in your dog's usual bed, or in the car or wherever you wish him to settle down. With the command 'on your bed', he knows to go to that blanket wherever it is and chill out!

Get your skates on

If your dog has got the idea of foot targeting (see page 103), this is a straightforward trick to teach. The same idea can then easily be applied to other objects, with the foot marker simply showing your dog where you want him to place his feet.

Choose a skateboard that suits the size of your dog – there are small ones that are ideal for smaller dogs. Take time to teach this trick so that your dog gains his confidence with the skateboard before you allow it to move.

1 Make sure your dog is confident with a foot target. Place it on the floor and give the 'on your mark' command (see page 103). Click as soon as he touches the marker with both paws and throw the treat. Repeat several times.

Skateboarding

As you teach your dog to skateboard, consider the surface you work on. A small dog may find it hard to propel a skateboard on a rough or soft surface and be put off trying. Instead, work on a smooth, shiny surface so that your dog can easily achieve the end goal. If you are worried about your dog being nervous of the skateboard tipping or making a noise, build up steadily and give your dog the chance to try. Dogs that are clicker-trained tend to become much more confident, as their natural curiosity is encouraged and rewarded.

2 Now place the foot target on the skateboard. Take care to position it so that the skateboard won't tip up and frighten your dog, and hold the skateboard still. Command 'on your mark' and click as soon as he places his paws on the target on the skateboard. Throw a treat. Repeat several times.

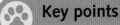

Key points

● Throw the rewards for your dog so that he gets off the skateboard and then has to return to it to earn another treat. This will build momentum and also make it easier to get the board to roll when your dog is ready.

● If your dog already understands 'on the ball' (see page 112) and 'on the stool' (see page 114), you can use the 'on the…' command to help your dog understand what you want more easily.

● Once your dog has got the idea of skateboarding, you are likely to find he favours one side for pushing. Bear this in mind as you send him to the skateboard.

3 Now remove the marker and see if your dog still places his paws on the skateboard. If he does transfer the behaviour, add the command 'skate', click and throw a treat. Practise this so that your dog understands the command. If he does not transfer the behaviour, do the exercise a few more times with the marker before trying again.

4 Now gradually introduce movement. Command your dog to 'skate', but do not steady the board. As your dog gets on, the skateboard will roll. Click and treat straight away. Gradually build up the distance a little at a time by withholding the click.

Tidy up time

This trick is made up of a sequence of several different smaller skills, each needing to be taught separately. Your dog has to be able to retrieve in order to be confident of picking up and dropping items on command (see page 104). Here, the different elements are taught and linked by 'back-chaining'. This is when you begin with the finish point of the task and build the sequence backwards, so your dog is asked to do a little more each time to reach the part of the trick he already knows well and associates with reward.

Choose your bin or wastebasket and what you are going to ask your dog to put in it carefully. Both need to suit your dog. The bin needs to stand a little bit below his chin height and be large enough for your dog to put his head into easily. If your dog can't reach the bottom of the bin, put a false bottom in it so that he can reach the item he is to pick up. For best results, choose 'rubbish' that is of a texture that your dog is happy to hold in his mouth. Here, scrunched up plain paper is used.

1 Position the bin close to you, between you and your dog. Place a treat in the bin and encourage your dog to get it. As he puts his head into the bin, but before he gets the treat, click. Let him eat the treat. Repeat several times to build his confidence with the prop.

2 Now place the 'rubbish' in the bin. Your dog is likely to go to investigate it – click as soon as he noses it. Repeat a few times.

Key points

● Let your dog think the problem through – you may simply wait for up to a minute without giving a command or clicking, unless your dog does something that warrants a reward.

● Concentrate on helping your dog to make the link between the bin and the paper.

3 Now re-present the 'rubbish' in the bin, but don't click when he noses it. By withholding the click, he is likely to try to mouth or hold the paper. When he does, click. Try to click and treat while he still has his nose over the bin so that when he drops the paper to get his reward it falls back into the bin. Repeat a few times.

⭐ **Clicker clues**

Teaching tricks like putting rubbish in a bin with a clicker is easy as long as you give your dog plenty of thinking time. Think of your job as giving him clues to the final goal – with the clicker, you are in effect saying 'yes, you're getting warmer'. When you do not click, you are telling him 'keep on trying and you'll get there in a minute'. Once a dog understands what the clicker means, it has just as much power by being withheld. It is a vital tool when you want to prolong or refine a behaviour or shape it by small progressive steps into another, different move.

4 Now place the 'rubbish' beside the bin and let your dog start to work out what you want. Click and treat when he noses or picks up the paper to begin with. Then withhold the click so that he has to try new things to get a reward. Click and treat for any action that will help shape the final task – for example, picking up the paper and taking a step towards the bin or simply putting his head in the bin again.

5 Gradually your dog will make the connection between being rewarded for putting his nose in the bin and for picking up the rubbish. When he places the paper in the bin, click and give a 'jackpot' of treats. Now practise and add the command 'in the bin'.

Shop, shop, shop!

This trick is quite complex and uses many of the skills your dog has already learned. Before trying this trick, make sure your dog is able to retrieve (see page 104), go to a target marker (see page 103) and can perform the waste bin trick (see page 120).

You need to teach your dog five separate actions, which then have to be performed in the right sequence. To build up a trick like this takes time and practice – work on one bit at a time to avoid overloading your dog.

Choose a basket that has a broad base, to prevent tipping, and a high handle so that it is easy for your dog to get hold of, as well as getting items in and out. Before starting to teach the full trick, teach your dog to pick up the basket by its handle and to hold it.

Planning lessons

When teaching a complicated sequence, take a few minutes to jot down each move your dog will need to make. Each one will need to be taught – for example, just because your dog knows to go to the mat doesn't mean he knows how to bring something back from it. By writing each move down you can plan your lessons, teach the hardest elements of a trick first, and more easily identify the cause of any problems.

1 With your dog in a wait (see page 30), place the empty basket on your target mat a few steps away. Send your dog to fetch the basket. Click and reward once he has brought it to you. Practise until fluent.

2 Now ask your dog to hold the empty basket and walk with him to the target mat. Give your target command and then command him to 'leave' (see page 105). When he places the basket on the mat, click and reward. Practise several times.

Key points

● It is better to teach all the basket tasks first, as these will be the least attractive to your dog. By teaching them first, you will have already attached a strong reward significance to them when you introduce the shopping items. Most dogs will find these much more attractive to pick up and retrieve, without the basket.

● The target mat will help clarify to your dog where you want him to go and where to put the basket. In time, when the 'shopping' is introduced, the mat can be removed from the trick, as your dog will know to target the 'shopping'.

3 Send your dog, carrying the empty basket, to the mat with your target command. Once he is on the mat, standing or sitting, and holding the basket, click. Walk to him and reward. Practise and then try linking the three steps together.

4 Rehearse getting the shopping into the basket, using the same command and method as for the waste paper trick. However, this time place your 'shopping' beside the basket and reward your dog only for putting an item into the basket. Click and treat when your dog does any move closer to achieving the goal or gets the items in the basket.

5 Finally, teach your dog to carry the basket containing the 'shopping', first at heel and then by sending him to retrieve the full basket. Once he does this, try linking the whole sequence. Begin by walking with your dog and work up to sending him to the mat and completing the other moves at a distance.

It's showtime

With a whole host of smart tricks and moves under you and your dog's belts, you now need a chance to show them off, so why not have a go at heelwork to music or freestyle?

Heelwork to music is still a very new sport – it developed from a demonstration of heelwork that was set to music and performed by Mary Ray in 1990. The idea was to make dog obedience more appealing and accessible to the audience, plus emphasizing the rhythm and movement of dog and handler. The performance captured the imagination of trainers worldwide and a new canine discipline was born.

The first competitive events took place a few years later and the sport has since developed into two distinct disciplines: firstly, heelwork to music, or HTM, which is traditional obedience movements performed to music, with dog and handler remaining close together for the majority of the routine, and secondly, freestyle. This is the creative and dance-like routines where dog and handler can perform any moves they wish, frequently to a theme – like Mary's famous performances at Crufts. In both disciplines, the judges are looking for an impression of 'oneness' and good interpretation of the music.

Check out the competition

Before you head for the show ring, make sure you have good general control of your dog, basic heelwork and are able to perform some of the more basic moves, such as twists. In the UK, there are no stipulations for an introductory routine, but other countries specify the moves you should be able to perform.

Go and watch some classes to get an idea of the standard required and what sort of moves and routines other competitors are performing. Ask at your local dog club to see if they have an HTM enthusiast or instructor who can help you further. If not, try contacting your Kennel Club or one of the main HTM/freestyle organizations.

Peak performance

To make sure you give yourself and your dog the best chance in the ring, do your homework. Consider how your dog tends to move and choose music to suit. Aim to pick a tune that is well known but not overused. The music itself will often suggest moves, but draw your ideas out on paper to make sure they flow well and use all the ring space. Choose a simple costume to complement your routine but not overpower it and then just practise, and practise some more. Be warned though, the sport can be addictive!

Useful contacts

AUSTRALIA
www.webforall.com.au/dogs/index.htm

BELGIUM
www.dogsanddance.com

FRANCE
www.debra@obe-rythmee.com

GERMANY
www.dogdancing.de
www.hundeallee.de/html/dog_dancing.html

JAPAN
www.caninefreestyle.jp
http://home.p04.itscom.net/k-9dance
www.japan-dog-academy.com/index.html
www.pawfect.jp

THE NETHERLANDS
www.canine-freestyle.nl
www.dtcsport.nl

UK
www.caninefreestylegb.com
www.heelworktomusic.co.uk
www.maryray.co.uk
www.paws-n-music.co.uk

USA
www.caninefreestylemagicmatch.com
www.canine-freestyle.org
www.clickertraining.com
www.dancingdogs.net
www.worldcaninefreestyle.org
www.musicaldogsport.org

Agility options

If HTM is not for you, why not try your hand at agility? A dog who has good all-round basic training as well as jumping and weaving skills is more than halfway there already. As well as keeping you both fit, it's an ideal way of burning off excess canine energy – a frequent cause of behavioural problems. Almost any dog can have a go, whether just for fun or in competition. Most dog training clubs offer agility, so what are you waiting for?

Useful contacts

AUSTRALIA
www.ankc.aust.com/default.html
  Australian Kennel Council
www.adaa.com.au
  Agility Dog Association of Australia Ltd

BELGIUM
www.fci.be
  Fédération Cynologique Internationale

CANADA
www.ckc.ca
  Canadian Kennel Club

FRANCE
www.scc.asso.fr
  French Kennel Club

JAPAN
www.jkc.or.jp
  Japanese Kennel Club

THE NETHERLANDS
www.kennelclub.nl
  Netherlands Kennel Club

NEW ZEALAND
www.nzkc.org.nz
  New Zealand Kennel Club

UK
www.the-kennel-club.org.uk
  UK Kennel Club
www.ikc.ie
  Irish Kennel Club
www.scottishkennelclub.org
  Scottish Kennel Club

USA
www.akc.org
  American Kennel Club
www.usdaa.com
  United States Dog Agility Association

Index

Acknowledgements

With grateful thanks to
Sue Evans, Avril James, Kay Laurence, Jan Morse,
Gina Pink, and Beryl Rounsley.

Sports Connexion, Coventry CV8 3FL
02476 306155

Executive Editor Trevor Davies
Editor Emma Pattison
Executive Art Director Leigh Jones
Designer Peter Crump
Special Photography © Octopus Publishing Group Limited /Angus Murray /Steve Gorton.
Other Photography © Octopus Publishing Group Limited 17 top/Tim Ridley 8.
Production Controller Nigel Reed
Picture Researcher Sophie Delpech

Kizzy

Glen

Busy

Taz

Gypsy

Chester

Zoë

Mabel

Quincy

Rooney

Saffy

Bailey

Keya

Foxy